CÉSAR VALLEJO: A SELECTION OF HIS POETRY

CÉSAR VALLEJO
A SELECTION OF HIS POETRY
WITH TRANSLATIONS, INTRODUCTION AND NOTES BY

JAMES HIGGINS

FRANCIS CAIRNS

Published by Francis Cairns (Publications) Ltd

c/o The University, P.O. Box 147, Liverpool L69 3BX, Great Britain
and
27 South Main Street,Wolfeboro, New Hampshire 03894, U.S.A.

First published 1987

Selection, Introduction, Translations and Notes
Copyright © James Higgins, 1987

British Library Cataloguing in Publication Data

Vallejo, Cesar
   Cesar Vallejo : a selection of his poetry.—(Hispanic bilingual
   texts; 1).
   I. Title   II. Higgins, James   III. Series
861   PQ8497.V35

ISBN 0-905205-36-7
ISBN 0-905205-67-7 Pbk

Library of Congress Cataloging-in-Publication Data

Vallejo, Cesar, 1892-1938.
   Cesar Vallejo, a selection of his poetry.

   (Hispanic bilingual texts ; v. 1)
   English and Spanish.
   Includes bibliographical references and index.
   I. Higgins, James, 1939-   .   II. Title.   III. Series.
PQ8497.V35A6 1987   861   87-20924
ISBN 0-905205-36-7
ISBN 0-905205-67-7

Printed in Great Britain by
Redwood Burn Ltd, Trowbridge, Wiltshire

CONTENTS

FOREWORD

This anthology is intended both to serve as a text for students and to introduce Vallejo's poetry to the general reader. In view of the difficulty of Vallejo's work, I have endeavoured in the Introduction to provide guidance by commenting briefly on each of the poems included as well as outlining the poet's career and poetics. The texts of the poems are based on the first editions and on the 1968 Moncloa edition of the *Obra poética completa*, prepared under the direction of Georgette de Vallejo, the poet's widow. The translations are my own, but I have consulted those of Ed Dorn and Gordon Brotherston, David Smith, and Clayton Eshelman and José Rubia Barcia, as well as those contained in Jean Franco's *César Vallejo: The Dialectics of Poetry and Silence*, and I acknowledge my indebtedness to them. My main concern has been to convey as far as possible the sense and spirit of the Spanish, and to that end I have been obliged to sacrifice other considerations. The English versions, therefore, make no pretension to do justice to the poetic richness of Vallejo's originals.

INTRODUCTION

Peru's greatest literary figure, César Vallejo (1892-1938) is not only Spanish America's foremost poet but, arguably, the most important poet of the Hispanic world in modern times. Though he was not a prolific writer, his work has an emotional intensity and a density and complexity of meaning which give it a quite exceptional richness, and he evolved a radically new poetic manner which revolutionised poetry in the Spanish language. In many ways it is remarkable that such a work should have been produced by a writer from a provincial backwater of an underdeveloped country isolated on the periphery of Western culture, but it may well be that, precisely because Vallejo did not feel himself to be at the centre of the Western literary tradition and, indeed, felt that tradition to be alien, he was unhampered by conservative attitudes and stimulated to experiment. Be that as it may, he represents a new phenomenon, that of a Spanish American writer who no longer follows in the wake of the great European writers but stands on equal footing with them at the forefront of world literature.

Of mixed Spanish and Indian blood, Vallejo was born and grew up in the little rural township of Santiago de Chuco in the heart of the northern Andes, where he had a traditional Catholic upbringing. He was the youngest of eleven children and, though his middle-class family was relatively well-off by local standards, life was always something of a struggle for his parents, but, despite that, he enjoyed a secure and happy childhood in a warm and affectionate family atmosphere. In 1913, after beginning and abandoning university studies in Trujillo and Lima and after two periods of employment on rural estates, first as a tutor and then as a cashier, he moved to the departmental capital of Trujillo, where he took an Arts degree and went on to study Law, financing his studies by working as a schoolteacher. Towards the end of 1915 he entered into contact with the local intelligentsia, who encouraged him in his literary aspirations, and several of his poems were published in the city's newspapers. However, in the last days of 1917 he departed for Lima, prompted partly by the break-up of a love affair but mainly, it seems, by the need for a more propitious intellectual environment than that afforded by a conservative, traditionally minded provincial city. He arrived in Lima with few friends and little money, but by obtaining a post in a primary school he was able to continue his studies at the University of San Marcos and, since by now his name had begun to be known, he was soon moving in the capital's literary circles. His first book, *Los heraldos negros*, appeared in July 1919.[1]

Los heraldos negros is very much the work of a young provincial with a limited cultural formation. In his early days as a student in Trujillo Vallejo was an avid reader of Spanish literature and, indeed, wrote a dissertation on Romanticism in Spanish poetry, but his knowledge of modern literature at that stage did not extend beyond post-Romanticism and it was only after he began mingling with other aspiring writers that he widened his reading to embrace the Spanish American Modernists, the French Symbolists and Whitman, and even acquired some awareness of the latest European literary trends through an anthology of modern French poetry in Spanish translation and by browsing through the avant-garde journals that reached the local bookstore. Not surprisingly, therefore, much of the book has a decidedly derivative and old-fashioned ring to it, revealing a tendency to strike Romantic attitudes and betraying the marked influence of a by now outmoded Modernism in its use of pretentious literary language and imagery. At the same time, however, several compositions employ a simple, direct, almost colloquial idiom as Vallejo frees himself from literary influences and moves towards a style that is a genuine expression of personal experience and emotions, and in some poems, too, there are the first tentative signs of the new poetic language which he was to develop in his later work.

The best poems of the volume convey the disintegration of a traditional world. Thus, a sense of the break-up of the familiar, secure, ordered world of childhood underlies poems evoking the poet's provincial home. "A mi hermano Miguel", for example, movingly presents the death in August 1915 of his elder brother Miguel, the playmate of his childhood years, as a game of hide-and-seek from which he has failed to return. Likewise, "Enereida" focuses on the lonely figure of his frail, aged father, against a setting (New Year, summer) which represents the cyclical renewal of nature from which the individual is excluded and thus highlights the old man's approaching death, though here the poet allows himself to be infected by the optimistic mood of the season and shakes off gloomy thoughts by persuading himself that his father will live on through his offspring. In a different vein, "Ágape" mirrors the break-up of the childhood world by showing the departed poet stranded in the lonely isolation of an alienating urban context that is the negation of everything the family home stood for. The whole poem, in fact, is based on an ironic contrast between the title, which alludes not only to the love feast of the early Christians but to the family values embodied in the shared communal meal, and the text itself, which expresses not only the poet's feeling of isolation but, above all, the frustration of

[1] Most of the 69 poems were written in Trujillo in the years 1915-17. "Ágape" and "La de a mil" were written in Lima in January 1918. Many of the poems were revised.

his need to give, to be part of a loving, sharing community. Nonetheless, the values of the disintegrating family home were to remain very much alive in Vallejo's poetry. They do so in the form of a communal ideal, expressed in "La cena miserable" in the image of a lonely, hungry child waiting endlessly at table for the fulfilling meal partaken with the rest of the household. They also manifest themselves in a compassionate awareness of and concern for the suffering of those less fortunate than himself, as in "El pan nuestro", which voices his wish to atone for the guilty feeling that his existence is lived at others' expense. In time, too, they were to lead him to embrace Communism.

A sense of the collapse of a traditional order is also present in poems reflecting the general spiritual crisis of modern times. During his student days in Trujillo Vallejo came under the influence of positivist and evolutionist thought, and Los heraldos negros expresses the existential anguish of a young man no longer able to accept the religious beliefs in which he was brought up. Thus, "Espergesia" is a variant on the theme of the death of God in the modern world, attributing the poet's anguish to his misfortune in being born at a time when God was ill and, it is implied by the final punch-line, on the verge of dying. In "La de a mil", on the other hand, God is still alive but, like the ragged lottery-ticket vendor who has no say in the distribution of the prizes, he has no control over the universe which he is supposed to govern and defrauds men's expectations by his inability to live up to their image of him. And "La cena miserable" anticipates the theme of Waiting for Godot, depicting life in a world without absolutes as a meagre, unfulfilling meal and an endless, fruitless waiting for "what isn't owed us", for something more than the mere existence which seems to be all the human condition entitles us to. However, the full extent of the crisis of faith experienced by Vallejo is revealed, above all, in the title-poem, where we see him reacting with confused bewilderment to the gratuitous cruelty of life, shaking his head disbelievingly at the hardness of its blows, unable to understand or explain why they should befall him. Here the poet is confronted by a reality with which his mind is unable to cope. The traditional doctrines in which he has been brought up, with their assumptions of an ordered universe and a benevolent God, simply do not correspond to his experience of life. Nor does reason, the tool on which Western civilisation has traditionally relied to understand the world, enable him to explain that experience. But, more than that, the language which he has inherited does not equip him to define that experience, for he is unable to find words capable of expressing the pain inflicted by the blows and his attempts to describe it taper off in an exclamation of hopeless inadequacy. All of Vallejo's later poetry could be said to stem from this opening poem of his first volume. For the books which followed represent an attempt to develop a personal language which will faithfully express his experience of the world, a language which will enable him to define that experience and thereby come to terms with it. Ultimately, it is through poetry that Vallejo strives to cope with a reality which is otherwise beyond his grasp.

In the meantime Vallejo continued to move in Lima's literary circles and was combining his day-time work as a teacher with a bohemian night-life. In August 1918 he had suffered a great personal loss with the death of his mother, to whom he had been very close, and this was followed by a series of tribulations. In September of the same year he entered into partnership with two colleagues to take over the running of the school after the death of the director, but it soon ran into economic difficulties and there was dissension among the partners. At the same time a love affair with a certain Otilia, the sister-in-law of one of his partners, was punctuated by quarrels and it and the partnership broke up when he resisted his colleague's attempts to pressure him into marriage. Then, during a visit to Santiago for the annual festivities in July 1920, he fell victim of local politics when, in the wake of a drunken riot, he was denounced as one of the instigators and, after a period in hiding, he was arrested in November and spent 112 days in prison in Trujillo before being released, the charges unproved. In March 1921 he returned to Lima, where he again took up a teaching post. *Trilce*, his second book of poetry and one of the great landmarks of modern literature, was published the following year,[2] but it proved to be too new and revolutionary in its poetic expression for the conservative Limeñan literary establishment and it met with a cold reception.

Trilce did not emerge from a vacuum, of course. Despite his limited cultural formation, Vallejo did have a certain familiarity with contemporary literary trends and there is no doubt that he was influenced by developments in Europe. However, he was mature enough to assimilate that influence and, above all, he was encouraged and stimulated by the example of the European avant-garde to pursue his own experimentation and to develop his own poetic style, and to a large extent *Trilce* was written independently of what was happening elsewhere. Like most modern poetry, Vallejo's new poetic style is remarkably concise and elliptic, with the result that the relationship between the different parts of a sentence is often only implicit; it abandons traditional metres and verse forms in favour of free verse with its own internal rhythm; and, above all, it is a poetry whose logic is internal, with the relationship between apparently disconnected

---

[2] The title is a neologism, possibly a reduction of the adjective "triplice" (triple) or a conflation of the adjectives "triste" (sad) and "dulce" (sweet). The first interpretation would suggest that the book is a striving for an ideal state of synthesis associated with the number 3, the latter that it brings into confrontation the sadness of the present and the sweetness of the past.
Most of the 77 poems were written in 1919. LXV was written in 1918; I and XVIII in prison (November 1920-February 1921); XIV, XXX and XXXVI in Lima in 1921. Many of the poems were revised.

images functioning on the level of the poetic emotion. What is distinctive about *Trilce* is its extraordinarily original use of language. Vallejo confounds the reader's expectations by his daring exploitation of the line pause, which often leaves articles, conjunctions and even particles of words dangling at the end of a line, by his frequent resort to harsh sounds to break the rhythm, by employing alliterations so awkward as to be tongue-twisters. He distorts syntactic structures, changes the grammatical function of words, plays with spelling. His poetic vocabulary is frequently unfamiliar and "unliterary", he creates new words of his own, he often conflates two words into one, he tampers with clichés to give them new meaning, he plays on the multiple meaning of words and on the similarity of sound between words. He repeatedly makes use of oxymoron and paradox and, above all, catachresis, defamiliarising objects by attributing to them qualities not normally associated with them. Vallejo, in short, deconstructs the Spanish language in an unprecedented manner, and by so doing he breaks down accepted habits of thought and forces the reader to view reality in a new light.[3]

Like *Los heraldos negros*, *Trilce* expresses Vallejo's alienation in a world that has lost its meaning. That alienation is intensely felt, for it is born not only of an intellectual view of the world but also of a personal sense of inadequacy and insecurity. An emblematic text is poem III, a dramatic monologue based on an episode from his infancy. The parents have gone out for the day and, as night falls and there is still no sign of their return, the child Vallejo grows more and more uneasy. Frightened of venturing out with the elder children into the yard where ghosts prowl about in the shadows, and equally frightened of being left on his own, he sagely warns them to stay indoors and wait patiently for their parents to return, but while he is talking the others disappear and when he discovers that he is shut up alone in the dark house, he cries after them in panic. Much of Vallejo's poetry is dominated by that sense of childish helplessness, by a feeling that he is a boy in a world too big for him to cope with, and the poetic persona he most consistently adopts is that of a child stranded alone and defenceless in a dark, incomprehensible and menacing universe.

In *Trilce* the disintegration of the world of childhood is now complete, brought to a definitive end by the death of the poet's mother, but it becomes the stuff of a personal mythology woven around the family home and, in particular, around the figure of his mother, who is repeatedly evoked as the archetypal purveyor of love. Thus, poem LXV identifies the dead mother with enduring values which make her immortal. Addressing her as a kind of saint, the poet vows to undertake a pilgrimage to Santiago to receive her blessing and to place himself under her care, and he makes ready by purifying himself of egoism and trying to

---

[3] Though her interpretations of the poems are sometimes dubious, Jean Franco (pp.79-137) offers an illuminating discussion of the language of *Trilce*.

live up to the legacy of love which she bequeathed to him. The love which she incarnated still has validity as the only force capable of overcoming the cruelty and absurdity of life, it is implied, and he will once more enjoy her protection when other men learn to live by her "formula of love" as he endeavours to do.

More generally, however, *Trilce* is a lament for the passing of childhood in which the family home is evoked as a paradise lost. Poem XXIII, for example, recalls how the mother distributed biscuits to her children, nourishing them emotionally with her love at the same time as she gave sustenance to their bodies. In the timeless mythical world of childhood life was regulated by that twice-daily ritual, which had all the solemnity and significance of the Christian communion. But now the clocks of the historical world of adulthood mark the end of true time as they measure out the minutes and seconds that are but indigestible left-overs from that eternal, fulfilling past. Cast out of the childhood paradise, the orphaned poet must now fend for himself, struggling for survival in a competitive world where nothing is given freely out of love and everything has to be fought and paid for. In poem XVIII, one of a number of poems based on his prison experience, the prison cell becomes a symbol of that cold, unfeeling world in which he is now trapped. Since his mother is no longer there to succour him, the walls seem to take on the shape of dead mothers leading children down the slopes of the past, and they thus come to symbolise the barriers cutting him off from the idyll of childhood and confining him in unhappy adulthood.

This opposition between childhood and adult worlds and between the values they respectively represent also involves an opposition between provinces and capital, for several poems record the homesickness Vallejo experienced in Lima as a lonely immigrant from the sierra. Poem XIV, for example, summarises the reaction of the recently arrived provincial overawed and intimidated by the strange new world of the capital. Totally unprepared for the reality he encounters there, he is bewildered and overwhelmed by a city where the natural order as he knows it seems to have been turned on its head, and his arrival in Lima thus marks his initiation into an apparently absurd and senseless world. Likewise, poem XLIX expresses his loneliness and uneasiness as, sorrowfully wearing his newly acquired manhood like an ill-fitting suit trailing at the ankles, he confronts the moment of truth when he must fend for himself in the competitive commercial world of the city. And in poem LVI life, in this strange, intimidating city where he knows no one, becomes an empty routine of eating and working for no other purpose than to stay alive.

The volume also includes a number of love poems, most of them apparently inspired by Vallejo's affair with Otilia. In some, such as poem XXXV, the beloved combines the wifely with the sensual and seems to hold out the prospect of a secure and affectionate family life which would recuperate the lost world of childhood. Vallejo, however, was torn between the attractions of sexual relationships and rebellion against subjection to biological laws. For, influenced as he was by evolutionist theory, he saw the sole purpose of life as being its perpetuation and the sole purpose of the individual as being to serve the species. Hence, in poem XXX, while love affords a sense of physical well-being and an illusion of transcendence, it connects the lovers "to what we are without knowing it" and they are represented as mere sexual organs coupling for the purpose of procreation. Hence, too, poem V protests against the empty repetitiveness of existence, against the senseless process of reproduction symbolised in the final stanza by numbers which are also a visual pun on the mating drive of the sexes.

In *Trilce*, therefore, there is a constant conflict between the poet's aspirations as an individual and his subjection to the laws of nature and the conventions of society. Poem LVII shows him suffering the aftermath of a personal catastrophe which has shattered his hopes of achieving self-determined fulfilment.[4] Nursing his sorrows, he nonetheless remains defiant. His aspiration is to forge his own destiny, to pursue his own path to self-fulfilment, and he continues to resist pressure to conform to social norms. And though he is aware that freedom is an unattainable ideal, something impels him to keep striving for it, so that life becomes a question of holding on against all the odds in an unfair world where everything seems to reduce itself to the same senseless, undifferentiated mass. Even more pessimistic in tone is poem LIII, where man is seen as the prisoner of his human condition and condemned to perpetual frustration. For, trapped as he is in the temporal world, his longing for freedom and transcendence is continually thwarted as he keeps banging his head against the existential limitations represented by the 360 degrees of the circle and by the boundary which keeps shifting to block him and is like a baton conducting his life.

Vallejo's nostalgia for childhood is thus also a nostalgia for lost innocence, for his view of the world in *Trilce* is the disillusioned one of a man who can detect no meaningful pattern to existence. Thus, poem XLIX shows him estranged in an alien world and desperately searching for something that would make sense of his life. A complex reworking of the theme of the theatre of life, it implies that the actors of the human comedy are no more than empty costumes performing a role scripted for them and advancing like automatons across the stage towards the dressing-room of death where the meaning of their performance may or may not be made clear to them. And in poem LVI, as the poet fumbles his way through a daily routine that is empty and meaningless, he reflects on the irony that the love which engenders children condemns them to a lifetime of suffering in a world not made to their measure. For the oracle that once explained the enigma of life has fallen silent in modern times and all man can perceive are

---

[4] The actual circumstances inspiring the poem would seem to be the break-up of his affair with Otilia, occasioned by his resistance of pressure to force him into marriage.

disjointed fragments of a confusing reality whose overall coherence escapes him. Therein lies the general significance of the disconcerting poetic techniques employed in *Trilce*, for their purpose is to sabotage assumptions of order and design and to convey a sense of apparently meaningless chaos.

Trilce, then, shows man trapped in an absurd world which makes a nonsense of his assumptions of meaning and order. However, part of the volume's richness derives from the fact that it is a book of conflicting poetics, and Vallejo's concept of the absurd is an ambivalent one, for he seems to have been convinced that the apparently senseless chaos of life conceals a unifying principle which, by confounding conventional notions of order, is an absurdity from a rational point of view. *Trilce*, in fact, posits the existence of a super-reality from which man is separated by the habit of logical, rational thinking, which has conditioned him to accept too readily the limitations imposed by the so-called natural laws, and Vallejo coincides with, and even anticipates, the Surrealists in their attempt to develop a new mode of perception which would reconcile life's apparent heterogeneity and contradictions in a great, all-embracing synthesis. Thus, in poem LXXIII he makes a personal declaration of independence, asserting his right to be dangerously anarchic in his pursuit of self-fulfilment. For to draw closer to ultimate reality he must first liberate himself from the world's values, and, if the first stanza indicates that this is a painful process since it obliges him to confront chaos naked and unprotected, the reward is the authentic harmony of the absurd celebrated in the final lines. In poem XXXVI he adopts the stunted Venus de Milo as an emblem of his poetics, evoking her, not in traditional terms as an image of classical beauty, but as an image of a human condition characterised by incompleteness and by a striving to surpass limitations. He urges us to reject the conventional way of thinking, which imposes on a reality that is essentially irrational a rational order which is comforting but ultimately false, and to surrender ourselves to chaos, since it is only by embracing life in all its absurd irrationality that we can achieve the seemingly impossible feat of passing through the eye of the needle, penetrating beyond the barriers of the rational world into another dimension where chaos falls into place and contradictions are resolved. Central to this poetics is the new poetic language of *Trilce*, for it is intended both to undermine traditional concepts of order and to convey the notion of an absurd super-reality. Thus, in poem XXXVIII the latter is symbolised by an everyday object, the glass, to which are attributed qualities which are absurd in logical terms. The glass is potential food capable of satisfying our spiritual hunger when we learn to recognise it as such and to approach it in the proper fashion. It is implied, therefore, that the harmony of the absurd is all around us but that we fail to perceive it because we are conditioned to look at the world rationally and logically. Moreover, as the symbol of the teeth indicates, reason is incapable of grasping that harmony because by proceeding analytically it fragments life's essential unity. The glass which must be swallowed whole by a toothless mouth thus symbolises a super-reality which can only be apprehended intuitively by a mind freed from the blinkers of convention and reason.

While some critics would dispute the attribution of such a poetics to Vallejo,[5] the opening and closing poems seems to frame *Trilce* within it. I interpret poem I as a dramatisation of the experience of epiphany, when the poet is possessed by an ecstatic sense of harmony and plenitude.[6] That experience comes over him in the unlikely moment of defecating, the islands of the first stanza being simultaneously the excrement which he deposits behind him and fragmented intuitions of harmony which detach themselves from the formless flux of life and coalesce within him.[7] The second stanza communicates the experience by means of an extended seascape in which the poet's heart, invaded by harmony, is identified with the guano islands of the Peruvian coast enriched by the droppings of pelicans and gannets; the third stanza, referring to the moment before dusk when the birds' activity reaches its peak, brings it to a climax with the musical metaphor, the resonance of the last line, and the visual image of bigness conveyed by the typography; and the final stanza evokes the calm and well-being that follow the experience. Poem I would seem intended to stand as an example of what Vallejo was aiming at in the rest of the volume. Poem LXXVII, on the other hand, is a commentary on the book it brings to a close. Here, as in other poems, the storm is a metaphor of disorder and chaos out of which emerges the life-giving experience of harmony, symbolised by the rain, and the pearls gathered by the poet are the poetry which he has forged from those experiences. But Vallejo recognises that he has met with only partial success in the pursuit of his ideal. He is afraid that the rain might cease before it has penetrated him to the core, for in the depths of his being there lie "incredible vocal chords", dry and as yet untried, which require to be moistened by the rain before they can fulfil their function of celebrating the harmony of the absurd. These vocal chords are a symbol of the poet's potential which as yet has been only partially realised and which can only be fully realised by further contact with the absurd ideal dimension. Hence the last line appeals to the rain to keep falling till he is saturated and submerged in the ocean of a universal harmony.

[5] In particular Franco, for whom Vallejo's poetry is essentially demystificatory. For a fuller discussion of this poetics, see my *The Poet in Peru*, pp.109-22.

[6] This poem has been the subject of several differing interpretations. See Franco, pp.117-20; Higgins, *The Poet in Peru*, pp.118-20; K.A. McDuffie, "Trilce I", in A. Flores, ed., *Aproximaciones a César Vallejo*, II, 113-20; B.J. McGuirk, "Undoing the Romantic Discourse: A Case-Study in Post-Structuralist Analysis. Vallejo's *Trilce* I", *Romance Studies*, 5 (1984), 91-111; Neale-Silva, pp.27-41; D.L.Shaw, "*Trilce* I Revisited", *Romance Notes*, 20 (1979-80), 167-71; G.G. Wing, "*Trilce* I: A Second Look", *Revista Hispánica Moderna*, 35 (1969), 268-84.

[7] The context in which the poem unfolds would seem to be the crowded conditions of the prison in the coastal city of Trujillo.

Poem LXXVII thus suggests that this poetics will be carried over into Vallejo's later work. In fact, he was to abandon this type of poetry, renouncing the quest for transcendental experience in favour of political commitment.

After *Trilce* Vallejo published *Escalas melografiadas*, a book of short stories, and *Fabla salvaje*, a short novel, in 1923. That same year he travelled to Europe, a trip which he had been planning for some time but which may have been precipitated by rumours that in Trujillo the charges against him were still being investigated. He arrived in Paris with little money and few connections and ignorant of the language, and during his early years there he suffered great hardship. In the autumn of 1924 he fell ill and spent over a month in hospital, where he was operated on for an intestinal haemorrhage. However, from the end of 1924 onwards his situation began to improve. In 1925 he secured steady employment as a secretary in a press agency, the *Bureau des Grands Journaux Ibéro-Américains*, and shortly afterwards he became a correspondent for Lima reviews, writing regular articles until 1930 on the European political, social and cultural scene. Meanwhile, he had formed a wide circle of friends among the Spanish and Spanish American literary community and in 1929 he began living with Georgette Philippart, whom he had known for some time and whom he was later to marry. During this period he composed a number of prose poems, but the planned book never materialised and they were subsequently included in the posthumously published *Poemas humanos*.

In 1927-28 Vallejo underwent a personal crisis which led him to interest himself in Marxism. In the first half of 1928 that interest was interrupted by another serious illness, but in October he visited Russia to see Marxism at work at first hand and in September 1929 he made a second trip. From 1929 onwards he seems to have written little in the way of poetry. Instead he devoted himself to the study of Marxist-Leninist theory and became a Communist militant, but after being arrested several times he was expelled from France at the end of 1930 and moved to Madrid. Despite the extremely difficult circumstances in which he and Georgette found themselves in the Spanish capital, his residence there was a period of intense political and literary activity. He joined a Communist cell and he wrote a number of works of a political nature. Of these he failed to publish the short story *Paco Yunque* and to stage the drama *Lock-out*, but he had more success with the novel *El Tungsteno* and with *Rusia en 1931. Reflexiones al pie del Kremlin*, an account of his impressions of post-revolutionary Russia. In October 1931 he made a third trip to Russia and early the following year he returned clandestinely to Paris and subsequently succeeded in getting his residence legalised.

In the following years Vallejo had no steady employment and he and

Georgette lived in considerable hardship. However, his third trip to Russia seems to have filled him with fresh enthusiasm and once again he began writing poetry.

He also wrote *Rusia ante el Segundo Plan Quinquenal*, a follow-up to his book on Russia, and the dramas *Colacho Hermanos* and *Moscú contra Moscú* (later retitled *Entre las dos orillas corre el río*), but he failed to find a publisher for the book and the plays remained unstaged. With the outbreak of the Spanish Civil War he redoubled his political militancy, collaborating in the creation of Republican Defence Committees, writing propaganda articles, taking part in political meetings and teaching in workers' cells. He travelled to Spain in December 1936 and in July 1937, on the second occasion to participate in an International Congress for the Defence of Culture. These visits confirmed his fears that the Republic was doomed to be crushed, but he continued working on its behalf, hoping against hope that the inevitable might be avoided. In the midst of his anxiety he had an outburst of creative activity and in the latter months of 1937 he produced a substantial number of new poems and revised others. Meanwhile, however, the hardships in which he had lived for so long and the exertions to which he had subjected himself had begun to undermine his health, and in March 1938 he fell seriously ill and on 15th April died in hospital of undiagnosed causes. The poetry which he had written in Europe, including a collection of fifteen poems on the Spanish Civil War entitled *España, aparta de mí este cáliz*, was published posthumously by his widow in 1939 under the title *Poemas humanos*.[8]

The poetic language of Vallejo's later work is essentially the same as that of *Trilce*, with, if anything, an even greater cultivation of techniques such as oxymoron, paradox and catachresis. There are, however, two new developments which in a sense are contradictory. On the one hand, in many of the shorter

[8] The 1939 edition of *Poemas humanos*, edited by Georgette de Vallejo, consisted of 91 poems, some of them dated, together with the 15 poems of *España, aparta de mí este cáliz*. However, in the 1968 Moncloa edition of the *Obra poética completa* the poet's widow groups 19 poems written between 1923 and 1929 as a separate book entitled *Poemas en prosa* and groups under the title *Poemas humanos* another 76 poems written between October 1931 and the final months of 1937. She also alters the order of the poems on the grounds that the typescripts often refer to the date of revision rather than of composition. This anthology follows the order of the 1968 *Obra poética completa*. According to that chronology, "Hasta el día en que vuelva ..." and "Salutación angélica" would date from around 1932; "Epístola a los transeúntes", "Los nueve monstruos", "Me viene, hay días ...", "Sermón sobre la muerte", "Considerando en frío ...", "Parado en una piedra ...", and "Va corriendo, andando ..." from the period 1933-35; "Piedra negra sobre una piedra blanca", "Intensidad y altura", "Un pilar soportando consuelos ...", "La rueda del hambriento", "¡Y si después de tantas palabras ...!" and "París, octubre 1936" from around 1936; and "Los desgraciados", "El acento me pende ...", "Quiere y no quiere ...", "El alma que sufrió de ser su cuerpo", "Al revés de las aves ..." and "Ello es que ..." from the final quarter of 1937. However, it should be borne in mind that Mrs Vallejo's ordering and dating of the poems have been disputed, particularly by Juan Larrea (see *Aula Vallejo*, 11/13 [1974], 55-172).

For reasons of convenience untitled poems are identified by the opening phrase followed by three dots.

The poems of *España, aparta de mí este cáliz* date from 1937-38. A first version of "Masa" goes back to 1929.

poems and within longer pieces there is a noticeable return to more regular forms and patterns, which up to a point represent a "return to order" after the avant-garde experimentation of the previous book. On the other hand, the poems often tend to be longer, being for the most part rambling, inconclusive monologues marked by an increased use of reiteration and chaotic enumeration and in which the formulae of rational discourse are undermined by the abrupt twistings and turnings of the text.

Much of Vallejo's later poetry continues to express an experience of urban alienation and a feeling of inadequacy in face of life, for in Paris he suffered the same loneliness and insecurity as in Lima, aggravated now by the rigours of the European climate, his precarious economic situation and illness. "Piedra negra sobre una piedra blanca", for example, records a mood of black despondency in which he feels that everyone and everything are against him and he foresees that his death will take place on such a day. Death is referred to as something which he has already experienced, for this dreary day is but one of a succession of such days which are slowly destroying him, and no nearer to coping now than he was in *Trilce*, he can do no more than protest, like a defenceless child unjustly punished, against the world's victimisation of him. Likewise, "El acento me pende ..." communicates his uneasiness and foreboding as life becomes a nightmare in which, feeling himself ostracised by his fellow men and watched over and judged by unseen eyes, he senses that he is being dogged by some sinister menace.

Above all, *Poemas humanos* is dominated by a sense of frustration caused by the repeated thwarting of the poet's deepest longings by the limitations of the world in which he finds himself. In "¡Y si después de tantas palabras ...!" the contradiction between his inner vision of what life ought to be and the drab reality of what it is leads him to view existence as an absurdity. For if, after all man's striving for transcendence, he is to succumb to the soul-destroying, humdrum routine of day-to-day life, if the stars are beyond his reach and he must live in the midst of combs and dirty handkerchiefs, then, the poet declares, life is hardly worth living and it would be best if it came to an end. "Intensidad y altura" voices his frustration at his failure to give meaning to his life through writing. For the raw material of experience resists reduction to a coherent linguistic expression and as soon as it is translated into words, as soon as the cough (tos) begins to become voice (toz), it is dissipated and develops into something different. Hence, unable to immortalise himself in verse, unable to redeem a meaningless existence through literature, he turns for relief to the only form of creativity and immortality of which he is capable, the sexual coupling which perpetuates that meaningless existence from generation to generation.

In *Trilce* Vallejo found in the walls of his prison cell a concrete symbol of the limitations imposed on him by a world which thwarted his aspirations to a full and satisfying life. In *Poemas humanos* those limitations assume the form of the trivia of domestic routine. Thus, in "Ello es que . . ." his prison is now the house where he repeats the same inconsequential acts day after day in an endless cycle of futility. Nonetheless, that routine does at least enable him to impose a certain order on his life and thereby to hold his despair in check. For he is gripped by an anguished sense of the utter absurdity of his empty existence and can see no way out of the suffering that is the common lot of humanity. This Sunday, on which he shares with the rest of mankind the role of sacrificial victim of the universal Mass, is but a vestige of a Christian message of salvation that has lost its validity, but he cannot conceive that Monday would really be any different, that any new creed would fundamentally alter the human condition.

With a weary sense of frustration which is often disguised by a self-deprecating irony, Vallejo repeatedly observes the absurdity of life in his own being. For while his spirit holds up to him a vision of a higher life, his experience of hunger and illness provides him with confirmation of evolutionist theory by bringing home to him the extent to which his existence is lived on an elemental, animal level, through that frail, decaying body of his which constantly demands satisfaction of its appetites and keeps breaking down under the effects of illness and age. "Epístola a los transeúntes", which seems to refer to his recovery after a period of illness, describes his daily life as the elemental routine of an animal, in which each morning he goes out fearfully to engage in the daily struggle for survival, cowering before the world like a hunted rabbit, and at night returns to the safety of his burrow to relax with the bloated contentment of a sleeping elephant. Mimicking the words of Christ (". . . this is my body . . . this is my blood . . .") as he surveys his person, he feels completely dominated by the immense mass of his body, which remains firmly anchored to the ground and refuses to raise him to the heights of a spiritually satisfying existence, and he sees his testicles as being the "bible" wherein the essential truths of life are contained. Looking ahead to his death, he presents it as merely the disintegration of that same body, as the end of a life in which nothing has been achieved, in which the shattered lamp of his ideals has been swallowed by the insatiable demands of the flesh. In the meantime, however, as his body recuperates from illness, he too forces himself to put a brave face on things as he resumes the unsatisfactory course of his life.

Hence "Quiere y no quiere . . ." expresses an ambivalent attitude towards life as the poet simultaneously clings to unsatisfactory existence and rejects the human condition as intolerable. With wry humour he tells himself that he ought to be satisfied with the gift of life and not be so ungrateful as to expect to understand it as well, but he is unable to keep up that posture for long and ends by categorically denying that there is anything heroic or beautiful about life and affirming instead that it is a source of continual anguish. That anguish was to become more acute as Vallejo's frail health made him increasingly conscious of the nearness of death. Thus, "Sermón sobre la muerte" is a tormented meditation in which death is seen as an advancing army sweeping everything before it and making a mockery of all human activities and values. Here the poet voices his determination to make a stand for life by resisting death with all the resources he can summon up, but "Un pilar soportando consuelos ..." concludes more pessimistically, with the acceptance that the only release from the terror of death is that afforded by death itself.

As well as expressing his personal existential predicament Vallejo's later poetry also registers his response to the political and economic crisis undergone by Western capitalist society in the 1920s and 1930s. "Parado en una piedra ...", a poem inspired by the spectacle of mass unemployment, evokes the plight of the unemployed worker and a world brought to a standstill by the absurd and tragic waste of human resources, and "La rueda del hambriento", "París, octubre 1936" and "Los desgraciados" portray the misery of society's down-and-outs, the victims of the crisis of the capitalist system. For Vallejo, as for many of his contemporaries, it seemed that what he was witnessing was the breakdown of Western civilisation, and a sense of a world disintegrating is conveyed by several poems in which, as man loses control of his world, the poet's personal inability to cope with life comes to be shared by humanity in general. In "Va corriendo, andando ..." the human condition has now turned into a nightmare in which panic-stricken man is engaged in headlong flight from the evil that pursues him from all sides. And in "Los nueve monstruos" the poet sees the floodgates burst open and suffering and misery spread with nightmarish rapidity, outstripping man's capacity to combat it and exposing the inadequacies of industrialised society and the liberal, democratic state as it turns a once-ordered world on its head and reduces it to chaos. Vallejo also saw in his own failing health an image of the critical state of Western man and in "El alma que sufrió de ser su cuerpo" he assumes the role of a doctor diagnosing the sickness of an ailing humanity whose spiritual malaise has grown progressively more acute as its traditional values have failed it. In "La rueda del hambriento" the plight of modern man is voiced metaphorically by the starving beggar who is left alone to brood on his destitution as his pleas for a stone on which to rest and bread to appease his hunger go unanswered. For, parodying the Lord's Prayer and St. Matthew's Gospel ("Everyone that asks, will receive ..." [vii, 8-11]), the poem is both an ironic comment on the death of God in the modern world and an expression of humanity's hunger for a new faith which would nourish it emotionally, provide a solid basis for existence and incorporate the alienated individual into a united human family.

Up to a point Vallejo found that faith in Communism. Both "Los nueve monstruos" and "El alma que sufrió de ser su cuerpo" are written from a Marxist viewpoint, the underlying implication being that Marxism offers the solution to the crisis confronted by Western society and to the spiritual malaise of modern man, and the ideal which animates his later poetry is no longer the super-reality of *Trilce* but the dream of a world transformed by socialist revolution. Many of the later poems are overtly political in character and others have political undertones, but Vallejo never subordinated art to politics and what makes his work superior to the bulk of political poetry is that it is not put at the service of an ideological message but integrates politics into it as an intrinsic dimension of his human experience and personal world-view. Poems like "Me viene, hay días . . .", where the poet is overcome by an urge to love so strong that it demands expression whether people want his love or not, indicate that Vallejo's Communism was born in large part of an emotional need to identify and share with others. And the presence of a deep moral sense behind his political convictions is made clear by "Hasta el día en que vuelva . . .", where it is affirmed that, though life is but a peregrination through an absurd world of frustration and suffering back to the void of non-existence which was its starting-point, the insignificant human animal nonetheless has a responsibility towards his fellows and can lend dignity to his miserable existence by fulfilling that responsibility.

A feature of Vallejo's political poetry is the application to a secular context of the language of Christianity, emptied now of its religious content but retaining its symbolic connotations to announce a coming redemption on earth effected by socialist revolution. Two types of working-class hero are the protagonists of that struggle. First, the destitute victims of an unjust society are portrayed in some poems as martyrs whose sacrifice promotes revolution by arousing consciences. Hence the wretched down-and-out of "Los desgraciados" is urged not only to summon up the will to endure another day of misery but also to accept his misery uncompromisingly by rejecting palliatives from the rich, for the spectacle of his wretchedness warms the poet and others to him, leading them to identify with him in his victimisation. His suffering is thus seen as a Mass, a sacrifice that will bring salvation, and the refrain running through the poem acquires an ambivalent meaning, suggesting not merely the dawn of another day of misery but also the approach of the day of redemption. Likewise, "Los mendigos . . ." depicts the beggars of all the earth's great cities as united in the cause of the Spanish Republic, for the war in Spain is but one front in a universal war against injustice and suffering, a war in which the beggars wage their own non-violent struggle, evangelising the world as the Apostles did before them. However, it is, above all, the working-class militant who is the hero of Vallejo's political poetry. Representing a new breed of man who has transcended the egoism of capitalist individualism to think and act in collective terms for the common good, he is celebrated as a Christ-figure destined to redeem mankind.

"Salutación angélica" mimics the Annunciation (Luke, i, 26-36) to announce to the Russian Bolshevik that he has been singled out from among all the men of the earth to assume the role of Redeemer. Though in most respects he is an ordinary man like any other, what distinguishes him is a spirit of brotherly love which he translates into action in the service of humanity, and his footsteps are, therefore, those of a man leading mankind towards a brave new future. Likewise, "Himno a los voluntarios de la República" voices the poet's admiration for the heroics of the militiamen of the Spanish Republic, workers and peasants putting their lives at risk to build a new world and leaving him, the vacillating intellectual, behind in the stone age of individualism as they advance into the future. And the parallel with Christ is made explicit when he directs to the militiaman a prayer based on the Lord's Prayer, in which it is implied that the militiaman is a victim sacrificed for the sins of mankind, which can become worthy and capable of redemption only when it follows the example of the worker hero.

Vallejo's hopes for the future are expressed, above all, in *España, aparta de mí este cáliz*, where the historical events of the Spanish Civil War are transformed into an enactment of humanity's struggle to build a better world. The Spanish Republic is presented as a symbol of the future socialist society in the process of construction, and the title-poem's repeated reference to "mother Spain" conveys not only a Spanish American's emotional identification with the mother country but a characteristically personal view of socialist society as a mother providing her defenceless children with loving protection and reproducing on a universal scale the atmosphere of the poet's own childhood home. *España, aparta de mí este cáliz*, in fact, constitutes a complement to *Poemas humanos*, for while the latter consists mainly of anguished monologues on the absurdity of the human condition, it looks forward to a redeemed future as Vallejo employs biblical language and imagery and adopts the tone of a prophet to announce the coming of a new Jerusalem brought into being by the sacrifice of a modern-day Christ in the shape of the worker militiaman, a socialist paradise in which a united humanity working together in solidarity will deploy the resources of science and technology to transform the conditions of life. Thus, lines 90-113 of "Himno a los voluntarios de la República" echo the prophecies of Isaiah to give a utopian vision of a future in which every form of evil will have been eradicated and men will live in harmony and plenty. And in "Masa", a poem modelled on the story of Lazarus, the resurrection of the dead soldier brought back to life by a humanity united in a common love is a parable of the eventual conquest of evil which will be achieved when all men learn to live by the values of the Republican militiaman.

However, Vallejo's political attitudes were much more conflictive than *España, aparta de mí este cáliz* would seem to suggest. "El alma que sufrió de ser su cuerpo", for instance, may be read as a dialogue between the poet and his *alter ego*, at the end of which the poet-patient rejects the diagnosis of the poet-doctor and, by implication, the Marxist remedy which would cure his sickness. The religious connotations of the title indicate that Vallejo was unable to free himself from metaphysical needs which a materialistic doctrine like Marxism could never satisfy, and the poem expresses the conflict of a man torn in two different directions at once. In the persona of the doctor he disapproves of his own metaphysical preoccupations as a symptom of decadent bourgeois individualism, but at the same time, in the persona of the patient, he experiences an existential anguish of which no amount of reasoning can rid him. That anguish was to become more acute as he felt life begin to slip away from him and "Un pilar soportando consuelos . . ." presents the ironic picture of a Marxist desperately turning to religion for comfort as he is seized by panic at the prospect of death. The poem shows him on his knees in a church whose pillars stand as a symbol of the moral support which religion offers to those who are about to pass through the dark door of death, and though the weary, disillusioned side of his personality looks on sceptically and dismisses prayer as a waste of breath, his thirst for immortality beyond the grave leads him to drink greedily from the chalice of hope. In the end he is too honest to delude himself, but, nonetheless, the poem illustrates the existential drama Vallejo lived through in his final years and the failure of Marxism to resolve it. Hence it is not surprising that, while he admired the party militants who devoted body and soul to the cause, he should feel himself incapable of such total commitment. Thus, in "Salutación angélica", after placing the Russian Bolshevik on a pedestal as the embodiment of socialist virtues, he confesses his inability to match his revolutionary dedication, for he is but an ordinary mortal subject to ordinary human weaknesses and there lurks within him a doubting *alter ego* which prevents him from seeing things with the Bolshevik's clear-sighted vision and from following in his footsteps.

Furthermore, it would appear that Vallejo was torn between an emotional need to believe in man and a jaundiced view of human nature which made it difficult for him to persuade himself that mankind was capable of improving its lot. These conflicting attitudes come into opposition in "Considerando en frío . . .", where the poet coldly and rationally analyses the human condition and accumulates evidence to prove to himself that man is a miserable animal beyond salvation, only to end up hugging the human animal in a fraternal embrace as his feelings get the better of him. Yet though Vallejo's instinctive solidarity with his fellows and his emotional need to believe were to triumph over his scepticism, his political optimism took a severe buffeting as the revolutionary movement suffered reverses in China and in Spain and the Russian Revolution lapsed into Stalinist terror. Thus "Al revés de las aves . . .", a kind of allegory of the political history of the 1920s and 1930s, evokes first the mood of euphoric optimism as mankind seemed to be on the verge of a new era, and then the bitter disappointment caused by subsequent events, which seemed to confirm the jaundiced view that humanity was incapable of changing its nature. And, for all its optimistic prophecies, *España, aparta de mí este cáliz* registers Vallejo's growing sense of despair as he confronts the imminent crushing of the Spanish Republic. In the title-poem he tries to shrug off that despair, recognising only with reluctance that the attempt to build a new society in Spain is doomed to failure and urging the survivors of the catastrophe to continue working and struggling to make that society a reality. The final image which emerges of Vallejo, therefore, is of a man who, as defeat and death stare him in the face, clings desperately to his faith in the ultimate and inevitable triumph of Socialism.

BIBLIOGRAPHY

This bibliography is necessarily selective. Further information is to be found in Flores, *Aproximaciones* . . ., II, 429-42, and *César Vallejo* . . ., pp.124-31.

1. VALLEJO'S WORKS

Obra poética completa (Lima: Moncloa, 1968)

Obra poética completa, ed. *Enrique Ballón Aguirre (Caracas: Biblioteca Ayacucho, 1979)*

Selected Poems, trans. Ed Dorn and Gordon Brotherston (Harmondsworth: Penguin, 1976)

Trilce, trans. David Smith (New York: Grossman, 1973)

The Complete Posthumous Poetry, trans. Clayton Eshelman and José Rubia Barcia (Berkeley: Univ. of California Press, 1982)

Novelas y cuentos completos (Lima: Moncloa, 1967)

Teatro completo, 2 vols. (Lima: Pontificia Universidad Católica del Perú, 1979)

El Romanticismo en la poesía castellana (Lima: Mejía Baca & Villanueva, 1955)

Rusia en 1931. Reflexiones al pie del Kremlin (Lima: Labor, 1965)

Rusia ante el Segundo Plan Quinquenal (Lima: Labor, 1965)

Artículos olvidados (Lima: Asociación Peruana por la Libertad de la Cultura, 1960)

Contra el secreto profesional (Lima: Mosca Azul, 1973)

El arte y la revolución (Lima: Mosca Azul, 1973)

Epistolario general (Valencia: Pre-Textos, 1982)

2. WORKS OF CRITICISM

Abril, Xavier, *Ensayo de aproximación crítica* (Buenos Aires: Front, 1958)

—, *César Vallejo o la teoría poética* (Madrid: Taurus, 1962)

—, *Exégesis trílcica* (Lima: Labor, 1980)

Aula Vallejo (Univ. Nac. de Córdoba, Argentina), 1 (1961), 2/4 (1963), 5/7 (1967), 8/10 (1971), 11/13 (1974)

Ballón Aguirre, Enrique, *Vallejo como paradigma (un caso especial de escritura)* (Lima: Instituto Nacional de Cultura, 1974)

Beutler, G. and Losada, A., eds., *César Vallejo: actas del coloquio internacional, Freie Universität Berlin, 7-9 junio 1979* (Tübingen: Max Niemayer, 1981)

Coyné, André, *César Vallejo* (Buenos Aires: Nueva Visión, 1968)

Escobar, Alberto, *Cómo leer a Vallejo* (Lima: Villanueva, 1973)

Espejo Asturrizaga, Juan, *César Vallejo. Itinerario del hombre* (Lima: Mejía Baca, 1965)

Ferrari, Américo, *El universo poético de César Vallejo* (Caracas: Monte Avila, 1972)

Flores, Angel, ed., *Aproximaciones a César Vallejo*, 2 vols. (New York: Las Américas, 1971)

—, *César Vallejo. Síntesis biográfica, bibliografía e índice de poemas* (Mexico City: Premià, 1982)

BIBLIOGRAPHY

Franco, Jean, *César Vallejo: The Dialectics of Poetry and Silence* (Cambridge: Cambridge Univ. Press, 1976)

Fuentes, Víctor, *El cántico material y espiritual de César Vallejo* (Barcelona: Anthropos Editorial del Hombre, 1981)

Higgins, James, *Visión del hombre y de la vida en las últimas obras poéticas de César Vallejo* (Mexico City: Siglo XXI, 1970)

—, *The Poet in Peru* (Liverpool: Francis Cairns, 1982), pp.24-45, 109-22

Larrea, Juan, *César Vallejo o Hispanoamérica en la cruz de su razón* (Córdoba, Argentina: Univ. Nac. de Córdoba, 1958)

—, *César Vallejo y el surrealismo* (Madrid: Visor, 1976)

—, *Al amor de Vallejo* (Valencia: Pre-Textos, 1980)

Meo Zilio, Giovanni, *Stile e poesia in César Vallejo* (Padua: Liviana, 1960)

—, et al., "Neologismos en la poesía de César Vallejo", in *Lavori della Sezione Fiorentina del Gruppo Ispanistico C.N.R.*, Serie I (Florence: G. D'Anna, 1967), pp.11-98

Monguió, Luis, *César Vallejo. Vida y obra* (New York: Hispanic Institute in the United States, 1952; Lima: Perú Nuevo, 1960)

Neale-Silva, Eduardo, *César Vallejo en su fase trílcica* (Madison: Univ. of Wisconsin Press, 1975)

Ortega, Julio, *Figuración de la persona* (Barcelona: Edhasa, 1970), pp.15-86

—, ed., *César Vallejo* (Madrid: Taurus, 1974)

Osuna, Yolanda, *Vallejo, el poema, la idea* (Caracas: Univ. Central de Venezuela, 1979)

Paoli, Roberto, *Poesie di César Vallejo* (Milan: Lerici, 1964)

—, *Mapas anatómicos de César Vallejo* (Messina-Florence: G. D'Anna, 1981)

Revista Iberoamericana, 71 (1970), special number devoted to Vallejo

Rodríguez Chávez, *La ortografía poética de Vallejo* (Lima: Compañía de Impresiones y Publicidad, 1975)

Vallejo, Georgette de, *Apuntes biográficos sobre "Poemas en prosa" y "Poemas humanos"* (Lima: Moncloa, 1968)

—, *Vallejo: allá ellos, allá ellos, allá ellos!* (Lima: Zalvac, 1980)

Vega, José Luis, *César Vallejo en "Trilce"* (Río Piedras: Univ. de Puerto Rico, 1983)

Vegas García, Irene, *Trilce, estructura de un nuevo lenguaje* (Lima: Pontificia Universidad Católica del Perú, 1982)

Visión del Perú (Lima), 4 (1969), special number devoted to Vallejo

Yurkievich, Saúl, *Fundadores de la nueva poesía latinoamericana* (Barcelona: Barral, 1971), pp.11-51

TEXT
TRANSLATION

LOS HERALDOS NEGROS (1919)

Los heraldos negros

Hay golpes en la vida, tan fuertes ... Yo no sé!
Golpes como del odio de Dios; como si ante ellos,
la resaca de todo lo sufrido
se empozara en el alma ... Yo no sé!

Son pocos; pero son ... Abren zanjas oscuras   5
en el rostro más fiero y en el lomo más fuerte.
Serán tal vez los potros de bárbaros atilas;
o los heraldos negros que nos manda la Muerte.

Son las caídas hondas de los Cristos del alma,
de alguna fe adorable que el Destino blasfema.   10
Esos golpes sangrientos son las crepitaciones
de algún pan que en la puerta del horno se nos quema.

Y el hombre ... Pobre ... pobre! Vuelve los ojos, como
cuando por sobre el hombro nos llama una palmada;
vuelve los ojos locos, y todo lo vivido   15
se empoza, como charco de culpa, en la mirada.

Hay golpes en la vida, tan fuertes ... Yo no sé!

2

THE BLACK HERALDS (1919)

The Black Heralds

There are blows in life, so hard . . . I don't know!
Blows as if from the hatred of God; as if in the face of them
the backwash of everything we'd suffered
had welled up in the soul . . . I don't know!

They're rare; but they're real enough . . . They open dark weals
on the toughest face and on the stoutest back.
They're maybe the steeds of barbarous attilas;
or the black heralds sent by Death.

They are the falling low of the Christs of the soul,
of some adorable faith blasphemed by Destiny.
Those bloody blows are the crackling
of a loaf that burns on us in the oven's door.

And man . . . Poor soul! He looks round, as when
over the shoulder we are summoned by a clapping hand;
he looks round in panic, and the whole of life
wells up in his eyes like a pool of guilt.

There are blows in life, so hard . . . I don't know!

3

Ágape

Hoy no ha venido nadie a preguntar;
ni me han pedido en esta tarde nada.

No he visto ni una flor de cementerio
en tan alegre procesión de luces.
Perdóname, Señor: qué poco he muerto!   5

En esta tarde todos, todos pasan
sin preguntarme ni pedirme nada.

Y no sé qué se olvidan y se queda
mal en mis manos, como cosa ajena.

He salido a la puerta,   10
y me da ganas de gritar a todos:
Si echan de menos algo, aquí se queda!

Porque en todas las tardes de esta vida,
yo no sé con qué puertas dan a un rostro,
y algo ajeno se toma el alma mía.   15

Hoy no ha venido nadie;
y hoy he muerto qué poco en esta tarde!

Agape

Today no one has come to inquire;
nor has anyone this evening asked anything of me.

I haven't seen a single cemetery flower
in so gay a procession of lights.
Forgive me, Lord: I have died so little!

This evening all of them, they all go past
without asking or wanting anything of me.

And I don't know what it is they've forgotten that feels
wrong in my hands, like a thing that's someone else's.

I've come to the front door
and I feel like shouting out to them all:
If you're missing something, here it is!

For every evening of this life
there's no knowing how many doors are slammed in a face
and my soul takes hold of something not mine.

Today no one has come;
and this evening I've died so little!

La de a mil

El suertero que grita "La de a mil",
contiene no sé qué fondo de Dios.
Pasan todos los labios. El hastío
despunta en una arruga su yanó.
Pasa el suertero que atesora, acaso   5
nominal, como Dios,
entre panes tantálicos, humana
impotencia de amor.

Yo le miro al andrajo. Y él pudiera
darnos el corazón;   10
pero la suerte aquella que en sus manos
aporta, pregonando en alta voz,
como un pájaro cruel, irá a parar
adonde no lo sabe ni lo quiere
este bohemio dios.   15

Y digo en este viernes tibio que anda
a cuestas bajo el sol:
¡por qué se habrá vestido de suertero
la voluntad de Dios!

The title refers to the cry of the lottery-ticket vendors. 1000 *soles* was the big prize of the period.
1/5.   A *suertero* is a lottery-ticket vendor, but the poem also exploits the literal meaning of the
        word (bringer of luck).
4.   *yanó*: a substantivised version of "¡Ya no!", an exclamation of irritation or weariness.

The Big One

The lottery man shouting "Here's the big one!"
has within him I don't know what depths of God.

All the lips go past. Tedium
blunts its nomore with a pucker.
The luck-bringer goes past, perhaps
nominal, like God,
hoarding, amongst tantalising loaves,
human impotence of love.

I look at him in his rags. And he could
bestow his heart on us;
but the luck which he holds in his hands,
crying at the top of his voice,
like some cruel bird, will end up
somewhere unknown and unwished
by this bohemian god.

And I ask on this tepid Friday that rides
our shoulders beneath the sun:
why would the will of God
assume the guise of a lottery man!

El pan nuestro

Se bebe el desayuno . . . Húmeda tierra
de cementerio huele a sangre amada.
Ciudad de invierno . . . La mordaz cruzada
de una carreta que arrastrar parece
una emoción de ayuno encadenada!   5

Se quisiera tocar todas las puertas,
y preguntar por no sé quién; y luego
ver a los pobres, y, llorando quedos,
dar pedacitos de pan fresco a todos.
Y saquear a los ricos sus viñedos   10
con las dos manos santas
que a un golpe de luz
volaron desclavadas de la Cruz!

Pestaña matinal, no os levantéis!
¡El pan nuestro de cada día dánoslo,   15
Señor . . .!

Todos mis huesos son ajenos;
yo talvez los robé!
Yo vine a darme lo que acaso estuvo
asignado para otro;   20
y pienso que, si no hubiera nacido,
otro pobre tomara este café!
Yo soy un mal ladrón . . . A dónde iré!

Y en esta hora fría, en que la tierra
trasciende a polvo humano y es tan triste,   25
quisiera yo tocar todas las puertas,
y suplicar a no sé quién, perdón,
y hacerle pedacitos de pan fresco
aquí, en el horno de mi corazón . . .!

Our Daily Bread

One drinks breakfast ... Damp cemetery earth
gives off the smell of the blood of loved ones.
City in winter ... The mordant passing
of a cart which seems to drag behind it
an enchained emotion of fasting!

One would like to knock on every door
and ask for I don't know whom; and then
to visit the poor and, weeping softly,
give out morsels of fresh bread to them all.
And to sack the vineyards of the rich
with the two holy hands
which in a flash of light
flew unnailed from the Cross!

Morning eye, don't wake up!
Give us our daily bread,
Lord ...!

Every bone in my body belongs to another;
maybe I stole them!
I came to take what was maybe
meant for someone else;
and it occurs to me that if I hadn't been born,
some other poor wretch would be drinking this coffee!
I'm a wicked thief ... Where am I to go!

And at this cold hour, when the earth
reeks of human dust and is so sad,
I would like to knock on every door
and beg forgiveness of I don't know whom,
and make him morsels of fresh bread
here, in the oven of my heart ...!

La cena miserable

Hasta cuándo estaremos esperando lo que
no se nos debe . . . Y en qué recodo estiraremos
nuestra pobre rodilla para siempre! Hasta cuándo
la cruz que nos alienta no detendrá sus remos.

Hasta cuándo la Duda nos brindará blasones   5
por haber padecido . . .
                        Ya nos hemos sentado
mucho a la mesa, con la amargura de un niño
que a media noche, llora de hambre, desvelado . . .

Y cuándo nos veremos con los demás, al borde   10
de una mañana eterna, desayunados todos.
Hasta cuándo este valle de lágrimas, a donde
yo nunca dije que me trajeran.
                        De codos
todo bañado en llanto, repito cabizbajo   15
y vencido: hasta cuándo la cena durará.

Hay alguien que ha bebido mucho, y se burla,
y acerca y aleja de nosotros, como negra cuchara
de amarga esencia humana, la tumba . . .
                        Y menos sabe   20
ese oscuro hasta cuándo la cena durará!

The Miserable Supper

How long must we wait for what
isn't owed us ... And round what bend in the road
will we stretch out our poor old knee forever! How long
before the cross that keeps us going ships its oars.

How long will Doubt confer honours on us
for having suffered ...
                    We've been sitting .
a long time now at table, with the bitterness of a child
who at midnight sobs with hunger, unable to sleep ...

And when will we be with the others, on the verge
of an eternal morning, breakfasted all of us.
How long this vale of tears, where
I never asked them to bring me.
                    Head in my hands,
my face bathed in tears, I repeat, downcast
and defeated: how long will the supper last.

There's someone who's drunk a lot and makes fun of us,
bringing the tomb near and pulling it away again,
like a black spoon of bitter human essence ...
                    and he knows even less,
that dark fellow, how long the supper will last!

LOS HERALDOS NEGROS

A mi hermano Miguel

In memoriam

Hermano, hoy estoy en el poyo de la casa,
donde nos haces una falta sin fondo!
Me acuerdo que jugábamos esta hora, y que mamá
nos acariciaba: "Pero, hijos ..."

Ahora yo me escondo,   5
como antes, todas estas oraciones
vespertinas, y espero que tú no des conmigo.
Por la sala, el zaguán, los corredores.
Después, te ocultas tú, y yo no doy contigo.
Me acuerdo que nos hacíamos llorar,   10
hermano, en aquel juego.

Miguel, tú te escondiste
una noche de agosto, al alborear;
pero, en vez de ocultarte riendo, estabas triste.
Y tu gemelo corazón de esas tardes   15
extintas se ha aburrido de no encontrarte. Y ya
cae sombra en el alma.

Oye, hermano, no tardes
en salir. Bueno? Puede inquietarse mamá.

To My Brother Miguel

In memoriam

Brother, today I'm sitting on the bench outside the house,
where there's no end to how much we miss you!
I remember that we used to play together at this time of day,
and Mummy would caress us: "But, children . . ."

Now I go off and hide,
as I did before, every evening
at prayer-time, and hope that you won't find me.
Through the drawing-room, the hall, the corridors.
Afterwards, it's your turn to hide, and I can't find you.
I remember that we made each other cry,
brother, with that game of ours.

Miguel, you went and hid
one August night, at first light;
but instead of laughing when you disappeared, you were sad.
And your twin heart of those extinct
evenings has got fed up with not finding you. And now
darkness is falling in the soul.

Listen, brother, don't be too long
in coming out, alright? Mummy might get worried.

Father phys- frail. Spirit. alive.   3 periods of time — 2nd is gov
gs., is fruit told,
is dead.

LOS HERALDOS NEGROS

Enereida

*Remove
Positive imagery in poem (quite untypical) of early Vallejo
but not untypical of later collection*

Mi padre, apenas,
en la mañana pajarina, pone
sus setentiocho años, sus setentiocho *metaphor*
ramos de invierno a solear.
El cementerio de Santiago, untado   5
en alegre año nuevo, está a la vista.
Cuántas veces sus pasos cortaron hacia él, — *his friends have died*
y tornaron de algún entierro humilde.

Hoy hace mucho tiempo que mi padre no sale! — *frail*
neog. — Una broma de niños se desbanda.   10
*Sort of —
strange use of
lang.*
Otras veces le hablaba a mi madre
de impresiones urbanas, de política;
y hoy, apoyado en su bastón ilustre — *majestic image*
que sonara mejor en los años de la Gobernación,
mi padre está desconocido, frágil,   15
mi padre es una víspera.
Lleva, trae, abstraído, reliquias, cosas,
recuerdos, sugerencias. — *isolated, can't communicate*
La mañana apacible le acompaña
con sus alas blancas de hermana de caridad.   20

Día eterno es éste, día ingenuo, infante, *it use as adj. it a use outside of
coral, oracional;   normal gram. category*
se corona el tiempo de palomas,
y el futuro se puebla
de caravanas de inmortales rosas.   25
Padre, aún sigue todo despertando; *his
es enero que canta, es tu amor *love will carry on*
que resonando va en la Eternidad. *he will live through love he gave.*
Aún reirás de tus pequeñuelos, — *life through kids*
y habrá bulla triunfal en los Vacíos.   30

The title is a neologism conflating "enero" (January) and "La Eneida" (The Aeneid). The poem
echoes Virgil in its bucolic tone and in the theme of renewal and rebirth. It is to be remembered that in
Peru January is a summer month.

Summer/day victorious of winter/night?

14

January Song

neologisms — coining new words, es - marauma pajarica

My father, *ar 'full of birds' (lots present)*
this bird-like morning, just manages
to put his seventy-eight years, his seventy-eight
winter branches out to sun.
Santiago's cemetery, anointed
with joyful New Year, lies within sight.
How often his footsteps made track towards it,
and came back from some humble burial.

structure /metrics
free verse
mostly versor llanos
sounds tail off -

Today it's been a long time since my father went out!
A band of joking children disperses.

Other times he used to talk to my mother
about his impressions of the town, about politics;
and today, leaning on that famous stick of his
that carried greater prestige in his years as governor,
my father is unrecognisable, frail,
my father is an eve of something.
Absent-mindedly he takes away and brings back relics, objects,
memories, suggestions.
The peaceful morning keeps him company
with its sister of mercy's white wings.

It's an eternal day is this, an ingenuous infant of a day,
choral, prayerful;
time is crowned with doves
and the future is peopled
with caravans of immortal roses.
Father, everything still goes on awakening;
it's January that's singing, it's your love
echoing down through Eternity.
You'll still be laughing at your little ones,
and there'll be a triumphal hullabaloo in the Voids.

13-14. Vallejo's father was for a time governor of the district of Santiago. The stick is the
governor's symbol of authority.
14. *sonara mejor*: literally, "sounded better", "had greater resonance". In Peruvian Spanish the
imperfect subjunctive in −ara often has the value of a preterite.

Aún será año nuevo. Habrá empanadas;
y yo tendré hambre, cuando toque a misa
en el beato campanario   *miel - honey - a made up word?*
el buen ciego mélico con quien
departieron mis sílabas escolares y frescas,   35
mi inocencia rotunda.
Y cuando la mañana llena de gracia,
desde sus senos de tiempo
que son dos renuncias, dos avances de amor
que se tienden y ruegan infinito, eterna vida,   40
cante, y eche a volar Verbos plurales,
jirones de tu ser,
a la borda de sus alas blancas
de hermana de caridad ¡oh, padre mío!

34-35. Santiago Crebilleros Paredes, the blind bell-ringer of the church in Santiago, was extremely popular with the local children, whom he used to amuse by telling them stories.

Impenetrable - make sense intuitively not conceptually - hermetic quality

Espergesia *(Esperanzanza / Genesis)*

lack of relig. faith / + personal crisis loneliness

blasphemous to X reader
Yo nací un día
que Dios estuvo enfermo.   *no hope for individual when God cant cope*

guilty individual
Todos saben que vivo,
que soy malo; y no saben   *but dont know the deep truth / the ½ of it - is he even more malo*
del diciembre de ese enero.   *- beginning of Gods illness*   5
Pues yo nací un día
que Dios estuvo enfermo.   *why these months beginning/end despair/hope*

limitations
Hay un vacío
en mi aire metafísico
que nadie ha de palpar:
el claustro de un silencio — *assonantal rhyme?*   10
que habló a flor de fuego. — *curious   a flor de - on surface again?*
Yo nací un día
que Dios estuvo enfermo.

The title is an archaic legal term signifying the passing of a sentence. The poet explains his plight by the fact that fate sentenced him to be born at a time when God was no longer up to fulfilling his role.

16

It'll still be New Year. There'll be patties;
and I'll be hungry when Mass is rung
from the holy bell-tower
by the kindly, sweet-spoken blind man who
conversed with my fresh schoolboy's syllables,
my rotund innocence.
And when the morning full of grace,
from its breasts of time
which are two renunciations, two advances of love
stretching out and pleading for infinity, for eternal life,
sings and sets in flight plural Verbs,
shreds of your being,
alongside its white wings
of sister of mercy, then, father, oh!

Verdict

I was born a day
God was ill.

Everyone knows I'm alive,
that I'm wicked; and they don't know
about the December of that January.
For I was born a day
God was ill.

There's a vacuum
in my metaphysical atmosphere
which no one will ever touch:
the cloister of a silence
that spoke at fire level.
I was born a day
God was ill.

LOS HERALDOS NEGROS

Hermano, escucha, escucha ...   15
Bueno. Y que no me vaya
sin llevar diciembres,
sin dejar eneros.
Pues yo nací un día
que Dios estuvo enfermo.   20

Todos saben que vivo,
que mastico ... Y no saben
por qué en mi verso chirrían,
oscuro sinsabor de féretro,
luyidos vientos   25
desenroscados de la Esfinge
preguntona del Desierto.

Todos saben ... Y no saben
que la Luz es tísica,
y la Sombra gorda ...   30
Y no saben que el Misterio sintetiza ...
que él es la joroba
musical y triste que a distancia denuncia
el paso meridiano de las lindes a las Lindes.

Yo nací un día   35
que Dios estuvo enfermo,
grave.

Handwritten annotations:

- is he catching someones arm
- I give up
- } no precise meaning — in poets life either
- exploring thoughts as writes
- impending doom
- confused metrics
- uncertainty
- La Luz = X
- accept mystery to understand Universe
- metapsychical boundaries undefined / transcendent
- punchline
- black humour — even though desperate
- Themes — Gods decay — sense of hoplessness then outsider v. world — trad values breakdown society can't respond
- associations of words are imp, opposites repetition.
- free style — distortion of rythum, breakdown of syntax — structure not first clear, 7 lines most So 2 syll line 'grave' is striking
- Jaan
- assonantal rythme

25. *luyidos = luídos.*

18

Listen, brother, listen ...
Alright. And don't go off
without taking away Decembers, *some despair ?*
without leaving Januaries. *+ leaving some hope ?*
For I was born a day
God was ill.

Everyone knows I'm alive,
that I masticate ... And they don't know
why in my verse there screech,
with a coffin's dark, uneasy after-taste,
chafing winds
unwound from the questioning   *— person asks + Sphinx answers*
Sphinx of the Desert.   *with riddle*
                                                    So hence 'preguntona'

Everyone knows ... And they don't know
that Light is consumptive,
and Darkness plump ...
And they don't know that Mystery synthesises ...
that it's the sad, musical hump
that from a distance proclaims
the meridian crossing from the boundaries to the Boundaries.

I was born a day
God was ill,
critical.

Images of illness/decay

Yo / ellos } the poet is a solitary
Yo / todos } misunderstood figure.
People only understand a bit
— post romantic view.
— access to deeper truth,
*   sensitive etc*

19

TRILCE (1922)

I

Quién hace tanta bulla, y ni deja
testar las islas que van quedando.

Un poco más de consideración
en cuanto será tarde, temprano,
y se aquilatará mejor   5
el guano, la simple calabrina tesórea
que brinda sin querer,
en el insular corazón,
salobre alcatraz, a cada hialóidea
grupada   10

Un poco más de consideración,
y el mantillo líquido, seis de la tarde
DE LOS MÁS SOBERBIOS BEMOLES

Y la península párase
por la espalda, abozaleada, impertérrita   15
en la línea mortal del equilibrio.

---

2.   *testar* (arch.), to testify.
6.   *calabrina* (arch.), stench of dead flesh; *tesórea* (neol.), from *tesoro*.
15. *abozaleada = abozalada.*

20

TRILCE (1922)

I

Who's making all that din, and won't even give
the emerging islands a chance to testify.

A bit more consideration
since it will be late soon,
and one will better assay
the guano, the simple treasurey fetidness
involuntarily bestowed
on the insular heart
by the briny pelican, with each hyaloid
squall.

A bit more consideration,
and the liquid dung, six in the evening
OF THE MOST SUPERB B-FLATS.

And the peninsula rises up
round the back, muzzled, fearless
on the mortal line of equilibrium.

III

Las personas mayores
¿a qué hora volverán?
Da las seis el ciego Santiago,
y ya está muy oscuro.

Madre dijo que no demoraría.   5

Aguedita, Nativa, Miguel,
ciudado con ir por ahí, por donde
acaban de pasar gangueando sus memorias
dobladoras penas,
hacia el silencioso corral, y por donde   10
las gallinas que se están acostando todavía,
se han espantado tanto.
Mejor estemos aquí no más.
Madre dijo que no demoraría.

Ya no tengamos pena. Vamos viendo   15
los barcos ¡el mío es más bonito de todos!
con los cuales jugamos todo el santo día,
sin pelearnos, como debe de ser:
han quedado en el pozo de agua, listos,
fletados de dulces para mañana.   20

Aguardemos así, obedientes y sin más
remedio, la vuelta, el desagravio
de los mayores siempre delanteros
dejándonos en casa a los pequeños,
como si también nosotros   25
                no pudiésemos partir.

Aguedita, Nativa, Miguel?
Llamo, busco al tanteo en la oscuridad.
No me vayan a haber dejado solo,
y el único recluso sea yo.   30

---

3.   See "Enereida", ll.34-35.
9.   *penas* (Am.), a shortened form of *almas en pena*, souls in torment.

III

What time are the grown-ups
coming back?
Blind Santiago is tolling six,
and already it's very dark.

Mother said she wouldn't be late.

Aguedita, Nativa, Miguel,
beware of going out there, where
ghosts doubled up with grief
have just gone past whining their memories
towards the silent yard, and where
the hens are still settling down,
they were so scared.
Better if we just stayed here.
Mother said she wouldn't be late.

Let's not fret any more. Let's go watch
our boats — mine's the nicest of the lot! —
which we played with the whole blessed day,
without quarrelling, as is right and proper:
they're still in the pool, ready and waiting,
loaded up with sweets for tomorrow.

Let's wait like this, obedient and with no
choice in the matter, for the return, the excuses
of the grown-ups who're always quick
to leave us little ones at home,
as if we too
                couldn't go out.

Aguedita, Nativa, Miguel?
I call out, I grope around in the dark.
Don't let them have gone and left me on my own,
and me be the only one shut in.

V

Grupo dicotiledón. Oberturan
desde él petreles, propensiones de trinidad,
finales que comienzan, ohs de ayes
creyérase avaloriados de heterogeneidad.
¡Grupo de los dos cotiledones!   5

A ver. Aquello sea sin ser más.
A ver. No trascienda hacia afuera,
y piense en son de no ser escuchado,
y crome y no sea visto.
Y no glise en el gran colapso.   10

La creada voz rebélase y no quiere
ser malla, ni amor.
Los novios sean novios en eternidad.
Pues no deis 1, que resonará al infinito.
Y no deis 0, que callará tanto,   15
hasta despertar y poner de pie al 1.

Ah grupo bicardiaco.

---

1.   The verb *oberturar* is a neologism formed from the noun *obertura*.
4.   *avaloriados*, a neologism involving a pun on *valor* (value, worth) and *abalorio* (bauble, trinket) and implying that the value supposedly derived from heterogeneity is in fact spurious.
10. *glisar* (Gallicism), to slip, slide.

V

Dicotyledon group. There overture
from it petrels, propensities to trinity,
ends that begin, ohs of ouches
one would think enhanced by heterogeneity.
Group of the two cotyledons!

Let's see. Let that be without being more.
Let's see. Don't let it spread outwards,
and let it think in such a way as not to be heard,
and colour and not be seen.
And don't let it slither into the great collapse.

The created voice rebels and wants not
to be network or love.
May the sweethearts be sweethearts in eternity.
So don't utter 1, for it will echo to infinity.
And don't utter 0, for it will keep so silent
that it'll wake up the 1 and make it rise.

Ah bicardiac group.

XIV

Cual mi explicación.
Esto me lacera de tempranía.
Esa manera de caminar por los trapecios.
Esos corajosos brutos como postizos.
Esa goma que pega el azogue al adentro.   5
Esas posaderas sentadas para arriba.
Ese no puede ser, sido.
Absurdo.
Demencia.
Pero he venido de Trujillo a Lima.   10
Pero gano un sueldo de cinco soles.

---

1.   The opening line is something of a puzzle. I have plumped for a translation interpreting it as
an elliptical expression along the lines of "[I put this forward] as my explanation".

XIV

Here's my explanation.
This lacerates me with earliness.
That manner of going about on trapezes.
Those toughs as brutish as they're phoney.
That rubber which sticks the quicksilver to the inside.
Those buttocks seated upwards.
That can't be, been.
Absurd.
Madness.
But I've come from Trujillo to Lima.
But I'm earning a wage of five *soles*.

XVIII

Oh las cuatro paredes de la celda.
Ah las cuatro paredes albicantes
que sin remedio dan al mismo número.

Criadero de nervios, mala brecha,
por sus cuatro rincones cómo arranca   5
las diarias aherrojadas extremidades.

Amorosa llavera de innumerables llaves,
si estuvieras aquí, si vieras hasta
qué hora son cuatro estas paredes.
Contra ellas seríamos contigo, los dos,   10
más dos que nunca. Y ni lloraras,
di, libertadora!

Ah las paredes de la celda.
De ellas me duelen entretanto más
las dos largas que tienen esta noche   15
algo de madres que ya muertas
llevan por bromurados declives,
a un niño de la mano cada una.

Y sólo yo me voy quedando,
con la diestra, que hace por ambas manos,   20
en alto, en busca de terciario brazo
que ha de pupilar, entre mi donde y mi cuando,
esta mayoría inválida de hombre.

17.   *bromurados* (neol.), from *bromuro*. Bromide was put in the prisoners' food to dull their sexual
      drive. It seems to be implied that the poet sees the slopes in his mind as he dozes under the
      effect of the sedative.
22.   *pupilar* (neol.), from *pupilo* (ward) and meaning "to watch over as guardian".

XVIII

Oh the four walls of the cell.
Ah the four dazzling walls
which without fail come out at the same number.

Nerves' breeding ground, evil breach,
how it wrenches towards its four corners
the daily shackled extremities.

Loving custodian of innumerable keys,
if you were here, if you could only see
how long these walls remain four.
Against them the two of us, you and I together,
would be more two than ever. And you wouldn't even weep,
would you, deliverer?

Ah the walls of the cell.
Meanwhile, what about them that hurts me most
are the two long ones which tonight
somehow have the air of mothers now dead,
each leading a child by the hand
as they disappear down bromide slopes.

And I'm left behind on my own,
with my right hand, which does for both,
raised aloft, in search of a tertiary arm
which, in the midst of my where and my when, will ward
this invalid state of manhood.

XXIII

Tahona estuosa de aquellos mis bizcochos
pura yema infantil innumerable, madre.

Oh tus cuatro gorgas, asombrosamente
mal plañidas, madre: tus mendigos.
Las dos hermanas últimas, Miguel que ha muerto   5
y yo arrastrando todavía
una trenza por cada letra del abecedario.

En la sala de arriba nos repartías
de mañana, de tarde, de dual estiba,
aquellas ricas hostias de tiempo, para   10
que ahora nos sobrasen
cáscaras de relojes en flexión de las 24
en punto parados.

Madre, y ahora! Ahora, en cuál alvéolo
quedaría, en qué retoño capilar,   15
cierta migaja que hoy se me ata al cuello
y no quiere pasar. Hoy que hasta
tus puros huesos estarán harina
que no habrá en qué amasar
¡tierna dulcera de amor!,   20
hasta en la cruda sombra, hasta en el gran molar
cuya encía late en aquel lácteo hoyuelo
que inadvertido lábrase y pulula ¡tú lo viste tanto!
en las cerradas manos recién nacidas.

Tal la tierra oirá en tu silenciar,   25
cómo nos van cobrando todos
el alquiler del mundo donde nos dejas
y el valor de aquel pan inacabable.
Y nos lo cobran, cuando, siendo nosotros
pequeños entonces, como tú verías,   30
no se lo podíamos haber arrebatado
a nadie; cuando tú nos lo diste,
¿di, mamá?

2.   There is a play on the literal and metaphorical meanings of *yema* (yoke/essence).

XXIII

Warm oven of those biscuits of mine
pure countless essence of childhood, mother.

Oh your four gullets, so astonishingly
ill-behaved with their whining, mother: your beggars.
The two youngest sisters, Miguel who died
and me still trailing
a lock of hair for every letter of the alphabet.

In the room upstairs you shared out among us,
morning and afternoon, from dual store,
those rich hosts of time, only for
us now to have left over
husks of clocks with hands stopped
on the dot of midnight.

Mother, and now! Now, in what cavity,
in what minute shoot of a tooth, could have lodged
a certain crumb which today sticks in my throat
and won't go down. Today when even
your pure bones will be flour
with nowhere to knead it,
tender pastry-cook of love!,
even in the cruel darkness, even in the great molar
whose gums pulsate on that lacteal dimple
which inadvertently moulds itself and bourgeons — you saw it so often! —
in the clenched hands of the new-born.

And so the earth will hear in your silence
how they all keep charging us
the rent of this world where you're leaving us
and the price of that never-ending bread.
And they charge us for it, when, since we were
only little then, as you would have seen,
we couldn't have stolen it
from anyone; when you gave it to us,
right, mummy?

XXX

Quemadura del segundo
en toda la tierna carnecilla del deseo,
picadura de ají vagoroso
a las dos de la tarde inmoral.

Guante de los bordes borde a borde.   5
Olorosa verdad tocada en vivo, al conectar
la antena del sexo
con lo que estamos siendo sin saberlo.

Lavaza de máxima ablución.
Calderas viajeras   10
que se chocan y salpican de fresca sombra
unánime, el color, la fracción, la dura vida,
     la dura vida eterna.
No temamos. La muerte es así.

El sexo sangre de la amada que se queja   15
dulzorada, de portar tanto
por tan punto ridículo.
Y el circuito
entre nuestro pobre día y la noche grande,
a las dos de la tarde inmoral.   20

---

2.   *carnecilla*, a swelling of the flesh.
3.   *vagoroso*, for *vagaroso*.

XXX

Burning of the second
all over desire's tender swelling flesh,
sting of restless chili
at two in the immoral afternoon.

Glove of the edges edge to edge.
Fragrant truth touched in the raw, on connecting
the antenna of sex
to what we are without knowing it.

Cleansing of maximum ablution.
Travelling cauldrons
colliding and splashing fresh unanimous shade
over colour, division, this hard life,
      this hard eternal life.
Let's not be afraid. Death's like this.

The sex blood of the beloved who moans,
all sweetness, at bearing so much
at such a ridiculous point.
And the circuit
between our poor day and the great night,
at two in the immoral afternoon.

XXXV

El encuentro con la amada
tanto alguna vez, es un simple detalle,
casi un programa hípico en violado,
que de tan largo no se puede doblar bien.

El almuerzo con ella que estaría   5
poniendo el plato que nos gustara ayer
y se repite ahora,
pero con algo más de mostaza;
el tenedor absorto, su doneo radiante
de pistilo en mayo, y su verecundia   10
de a centavito, por quítame allá esa paja.
Y la cerveza lírica y nerviosa
a la que celan sus dos pezones sin lúpulo,
y que no se debe tomar mucho!

Y los demás encantos de la mesa   15
que aquella núbil campaña borda
con sus propias baterías germinales
que han operado toda la mañana,
según me consta, a mí,
amoroso notario de sus intimidades,   20
y con las diez varillas mágicas
de sus dedos pancreáticos.

Mujer que, sin pensar en nada más allá,
suelta el mirlo y se pone a conversarnos
sus palabras tiernas   25
como lancinantes lechugas recién cortadas.

Otro vaso y me voy. Y nos marchamos,
ahora sí, a trabajar.

3-4. The programmes of the Lima race-track of the period were purple-coloured and extremely
      long. The lines are, of course, susceptible of a metaphorical interpretation.
9.   *doneo* (arch.), coquettishness.
13.   There is a play on the two meanings of *celar* (to watch over/to conceal). The beer referred to
      is thus both that which she serves to her guest and that contained in her breasts.

XXXV

The meeting with the beloved
so often sometimes amounts to a simple detail,
almost a violet race programme
that's so long it's hard to fold.

Lunch with her who'd be
serving up the dish we liked yesterday
and is being repeated now,
but with a bit more mustard;
the distracted fork, her radiant coquettishness
of pistil in May, and her ten-a-penny
blushes at the slightest trifle.
And the lyrical, nervous beer
overseen by her two hopless teats
and of which one shouldn't drink too much!

And the other charms of the table
woven by that nubile campaign of hers
with its own germinal batteries
which have been operating all morning,
as has been recorded by me,
loving notary of her intimacies,
and with the ten magic wands
of her pancreatic fingers.

Woman who, thinking of nothing beyond the immediate,
loosens her tongue and starts chatting to us
her words tender
as sharp, fresh-cut lettuce.

Another glass and I'm off. And this time
we really are going off to work.

---

17. *baterías* simultaneously conjures up images of artillery and of kitchen utensils (*batería de cocina*).
24. *soltar el mirlo* (coll.), to loosen one's tongue.

Entre tanto, ella se interna
entre los cortinajes y ¡oh aguja de mis días   30
desgarrados! se sienta a la orilla
de una costura, a coserme el costado
a su costado,
a pegar el botón de esa camisa,
que se ha vuelto a caer. Pero hase visto!   35

XXXVI

Pugnamos ensartarnos por un ojo de aguja,
enfrentados, a las ganadas.
Amoniácase casi el cuarto ángulo del círculo.
¡Hembra se continúa el macho, a raíz
de probables senos, y precisamente   5
a raíz de cuanto no florece!

¿Por ahí estás, Venus de Milo?
Tú manqueas apenas pululando
entrañada en los brazos plenarios
de la existencia,   10
de esta existencia que todaviiza
perenne imperfección.
Venus de Milo, cuyo cercenado, increado
brazo revuélvese y trata de encodarse
a través de verdeantes guijarros gagos,   15
ortivos nautilos, aunes que gatean
recién, vísperas inmortales.
Laceadora de inminencias, laceadora
del paréntesis.

Rehusad, y vosotros, a posar las plantas   20
en la seguridad dupla de la Armonía.

3.   amoniacar is a neologism formed by analogy with and as an antonym of anestesiar (to anaesthetise). Its meaning is "to revive", "to bring to life".
11.   todaviiza (neol.), from todavía (yet, still) and meaning "prolongs", "perpetuates".
14.   encodarse (neol.), to become an elbow.

Meanwhile, she slips
behind the curtains and — oh needle of my torn
days! — she sits down at the edge
of a seam, to sew my side
to her side,
to sew on the shirt-button
that's fallen off again. Did you ever see such a thing!

XXXVI

We struggle to thread ourselves through the eye of a needle,
head on, out to win.
The fourth angle of the circle is almost ammoniatised.
The male continues as female, by virtue
of probable breasts, and precisely
by virtue of all that doesn't flourish!

Are you there, Venus de Milo?
You dangle your barely budding stump
embedded in the plenary arms
of existence,
of this existence which yets
perennial imperfection.
Venus de Milo, whose stunted, uncreated
arm stirs and tries to become elbow
amidst green stuttering stones,
sky-rising nautili, yets
newly crawling, immortal eves.
Lassoer of imminences, lassoer
of the parenthesis.

Refuse, you too, to plant your feet
on the double security of Harmony.

15.   *gagos* (arch.), stammering, stuttering.
16.   *aunes*, a substantivised form of the adverb and meaning "potentialities", "that which has not
       yet come into being".

Rehusad la simetría a buen seguro.
Intervenid en el conflicto
de puntas que se disputan
en la más torionda de las justas   25
el salto por el ojo de la aguja!

Tal siento ahora al meñique
demás en la siniestra. Lo veo y creo
no debe serme, o por lo menos que está
en sitio donde no debe.   30
˘Y me inspira rabia y me azarea
y no hay cómo salir de él, sino haciendo
la cuenta de que hoy es jueves.

¡Ceded al nuevo impar
                            potente de orfandad!   35

Refuse safe symmetry.
Intervene in the conflict
of tips contending
in the most ruttish of jousts
the leap through the eye of the needle!

So now do I feel my little finger
superfluous on my left hand. I see it and think
it can't be mine, or at least that it's
where it shouldn't be.
And it enrages me and flusters me
and there's no way out of it, except by making
the reckoning that today is Thursday.

Yield to the new odd number
                              potent in orphanhood!

XXXVIII

Este cristal aguarda ser sorbido
en bruto por boca venidera
sin dientes. No desdentada.
Este cristal es pan no venido todavía.

Hiere cuando lo fuerzan   5
y ya no tiene cariños animales.
·Mas si se le apasiona, se melaría
y tomaría la horma de los sustantivos
que se adjetivan de brindarse.

Quienes lo ven allí triste individuo   10
incoloro, lo enviarían por amor,
por pasado y a lo más por futuro:
si él no dase por ninguno de sus costados;
si él espera ser sorbido de golpe
y en cuanto transparencia, por boca ve-   15
nidera que ya no tendrá dientes.

Este cristal ha pasado de animal,
y márchase ahora a formar las izquierdas,
los nuevos Menos.
Déjenlo solo no más.   20

XXXVIII

This glass is waiting to be swallowed
whole by a future mouth
without teeth. Not one that has lost them.
This glass is bread yet to come.

It hurts back when it's forced
and no longer displays animal affection.
But if wooed, it would turn to honey
and take on the shape of nouns
adjectivised by giving of themselves.

Anyone seeing it there, a sad, colourless
individual, would send it for love,
for the past or, at the most, for the future:
for it doesn't yield on any of its sides;
for it's waiting to be swallowed at one go
and as transparency by a prospect-
ive mouth which won't have any teeth.

This glass has passed beyond the animal,
and goes off to form the lefts,
the new Minuses.
Just leave it alone.

XLIX

Murmurando en inquietud, cruzo,
el traje largo de sentir, los lunes
    de la verdad.
Nadie me busca ni me reconoce,
y hasta yo he olvidado   5
    de quién seré.

Cierta guardarropía, sólo ella, nos sabrá
a todos en las blancas hojas
    de las partidas.
Esa guardarropía, ella sola,   10
al volver de cada facción,
    de cada candelabro
    ciego de nacimiento.

Tampoco yo descubro a nadie, bajo
este mantillo que iridice los lunes   15
    de la razón;
y no hago más que sonreír a cada púa
de las verjas, en la loca búsqueda
    del conocido.

Buena guardarropía, ábreme   20
    tus blancas hojas;
quiero reconocer siquiera al 1,
quiero el punto de apoyo, quiero
    saber de estar siquiera.

En los bastidores donde nos vestimos,   25
no hay, no Hay nadie: hojas tan sólo
    de par en par.
Y siempre los trajes descolgándose
por sí propios, de perchas
como ductores índices grotescos,   30
y partiendo sin cuerpos, vacantes,
    hasta el matiz prudente

---

15.   The neologism *iridice* would seem to be a verbal form of the adjective *iridescente*.

XLIX

Muttering with anxiety, my clothes
trailing with dejection, I trek through the mondays
      of truth.
No one seeks me out or recognises me,
and even I have forgotten
      to whom I belong.

A certain wardrobe, only it, will know
us all on the blank pages
      of the registers.
That wardrobe, it alone,
on the return of each faction,
      of each candelabrum
      blind from birth.

I can't find anyone either, beneath
this humus which iridesces the mondays
      of reason;
and all I do is smile at each spike
on the railings, in the mad search
      for one I know.

Good wardrobe, open up for me
      your white leaves;
I want at least to recognise number 1,
I want the point of support, I want
      at least to be aware of existing.

In the wings where we dress,
there isn't, there Isn't anybody: just leaves
      wide open.
And always the costumes climbing down
by themselves, from stands
like grotesque pointing forefingers,
and going off without bodies, empty,
      till the discreet hue

de un gran caldo de alas con causas
y lindes fritas.
Y hasta el hueso!   35

LIII

Quién clama las once no son doce!
Como si las hubiesen pujado, se afrontan
de dos en dos las once veces.

Cabezazo brutal. Asoman
las coronas a oír,   5
pero sin traspasar los eternos
trescientos sesenta grados, asoman
y exploran en balde, dónde ambas manos
ocultan el otro puente que les nace
entre veras y litúrgicas bromas.   10

Vuelve la frontera a probar
las dos piedras que no alcanzan a ocupar
una misma posada a un mismo tiempo.
La frontera, la ambulante batuta, que sigue
inmutable, igual, sólo   15
más ella a cada esguince en alto.

Veis lo que es sin poder ser negado,
veis lo que tenemos que aguantar,
mal que nos pese.
¡Cuánto se aceita en codos   20
que llegan hasta la boca!

20-21. These lines would seem to be an elaboration of the phrase *comerse los codos*, to suffer hunger, privation, unfulfilment (literally, to gnaw one's elbows). The sense appears to be that everything previously mentioned in the poem serves as lubrication to facilitate the process of gnawing the elbows, i.e. accentuates unfulfilment and frustration.

of a great soup of wings with fried
causes and limits.
And till it gets right down to the bone!

LIII

Who claims eleven o'clock isn't twelve!
As though pushed up by bidding, they confront each other
in twos eleven times.

Brutal bang of the head. The crowns
peep out to listen,
but without going beyond the eternal
three hundred and sixty degrees, they peep out
and explore in vain for where both hands
conceal the other bridge born to them
between verges and liturgical jokes.

Once again the boundary demonstrates
the two stones that never manage to occupy
the same position at the same time.
The boundary, the itinerant baton, which remains
immutable, the same, only
more itself with each swerve on high.

See what is without possibility of denial,
see what we have to put up with,
sorely though it grieves us.
How much is greased on elbows
which reach to the mouth!

LVI

Todos los días amanezco a ciegas
a trabajar para vivir; y tomo el desayuno,
sin probar ni gota de él, todas las mañanas.
Sin saber si he logrado, o más nunca,
algo que brinca del sabor 5
o es sólo corazón y que ya vuelto, lamentará
hasta dónde esto es lo menos.

El niño crecería ahito de felicidad
　　　oh albas,
ante el pesar de los padres de no poder dejarnos 10
de arrancar de sus sueños de amor a este mundo;
ante ellos que, como Dios, de tanto amor
se comprendieron hasta creadores
y nos quisieron hasta hacernos daño.

Flecos de invisible trama, 15
dientes que huronean desde la neutra emoción,
　　　pilares
libres de base y coronación,
en la gran boca que ha perdido el habla.

Fósforo y fósforo en la oscuridad, 20
lágrima y lágrima en la polvareda.

LVI

Every day I blindly rise
to work in order to live; and I take breakfast
without tasting a drop of it, every morning.
Without knowing if I've achieved, or ever shall again,
something that springs from the taste
or if it's just heart that on its return will lament
the extent to which this is the least of things.

The child would grow up sated with happiness
                    oh dawns,
in face of the sorrow of the parents helpless to avoid
wrenching us from their dreams of love into this world;
in face of them who, like God, were so full of love
they understood themselves to the point of being creators
and loved us to the point of causing us harm.

Fringes of an invisible weave,
teeth which ferret from neutral emotion,
                    pillars
free of base and crown,
in the great mouth which has lost its speech.

Match after match in the darkness,
tear after tear in the dust-filled air.

LVII

Craterizados los puntos más altos, los puntos
del amor de ser mayúsculo, bebo, ayuno, ab-
sorbo heroína para la pena, para el latido
lacio y contra toda corrección.

¿Puedo decir que nos han traicionado? No.   5
¿Que todos fueron buenos? Tampoco. Pero
allí está una buena voluntad, sin duda,
y sobre todo, el ser así.

Y qué quien se ame mucho! Yo me busco
en mi propio designio que debió ser obra   10
mía, en vano: nada alcanzó a ser libre.

Y sin embargo, quién me empuja.
A que no me atrevo a cerrar la quinta ventana.
Y el papel de amarse y persistir, junto a las
horas y a lo indebido.   15

Y el éste y el aquél.

3-8. The bohemian life which Vallejo led in Lima included occasional visits to opium dens in the Chinese quarter. These lines might suggest that the poetic persona is speaking under the influence of drugs.

9. *quien se ame mucho*: the opening phrase of a moralising cliché censuring self-love.

LVII

Cratered the highest points, the points
of love of upper-case being, I drink, don't eat, ab-
sorb heroin for the pain, for the limp
throb and in defiance of all correction.

Can I say that they've betrayed us? No.
That they were all good? Not that either. But
there's goodwill there, no doubt,
and, above all, being like this.

And all that he who loves himself! I seek myself
in my own design which should have been my own
work, in vain: nothing managed to be free.

And yet, who's driving me?
Here's betting I don't dare close the fifth window.
And the role of loving oneself and persisting, alongside the
hours and the undeserved.

And the this and the that.

LXV

Madre, me voy mañana a Santiago,
a mojarme en tu bendición y en tu llanto.
Acomodando estoy mis desengaños y el rosado
de llaga de mis falsos trajines.

Me esperará tu arco de asombro,   5
las tonsuradas columnas de tus ansias
que se acaban la vida. Me esperará el patio,
el corredor de abajo con sus tondos y repulgos
de fiesta. Me esperará mi sillón ayo,
aquel buen quijarudo trasto de dinástico   10
cuero, que para no más rezongando a las nalgas
tataranietas, de correa a correhuela.

Estoy cribando mis cariños más puros.
Estoy ejeando, ¿no oyes jadear la sonda?
          ¿no oyes tascar dianas?   15
estoy plasmando tu fórmula de amor
para todos los huecos de este suelo.
Oh si se dispusieran los tácitos volantes
para todas las cintas más distantes,
para todas las citas más distintas.   20

Así, muerta inmortal. Así.
Bajo los dobles arcos de tu sangre, por donde
hay que pasar tan de puntillas, que hasta mi padre
para ir por allí,
humildóse hasta menos de la mitad del hombre,   25
hasta ser el primer pequeño que tuviste.

Así, muerta inmortal.
Entre la columnata de tus huesos

---

9. *ayo* normally means "tutor", but here it also has the sense of the French *aieul* (grandfather).
    The chair is thus represented as an old man entrusted with the task of disciplining and
    educating a young boy.

12. The conjunction of *correa* and its diminutive *correhuela* implies that the chair is like an adult
    chastising a child.

14. The verb *ejear* is a neologism formed from *eje* (axis), by analogy with *sondear* (to sound),
    and meaning "to strive to get to one's essence".

LXV

Mother, I'm off tomorrow to Santiago,
to soak myself in your blessing and your tears.
I'm arranging my disillusionments and the rosy
sore of my false comings and goings.

Waiting for me will be your arch of astonishment,
the tonsured columns of your anxiety
that brings life to an end. Waiting for me will be the patio,
the downstairs corridor with its festive
mouldings and edgings. Waiting for me will be my grandfather chair,
that good old big-jawed heap of dynastic
leather, which just stands there scolding the great-great-grandchildish
buttocks, as strap to strapling.

I'm sifting my purest affections.
I'm axising — can't you hear the panting of the sounding-lead?
            can't you hear the champing of reveilles? —,
I'm shaping your formula of love
for all the hollows of this earth.
Oh if only the tacit flyers would make ready
for all the most distant ribbons,
for all the most distinct rendezvous.

Just so, immortal dead one. Just so.
Under the double arches of your blood, where
one must tiptoe so gently that even my father,
to pass that way,
humbled himself to less than half of man,
till he was the first little one you had.

Just so, immortal dead one.
Beneath the colonnade of your bones

18.   My translation interprets *volantes* as flyers, handbills spreading a message of love.
      Alternatively, the *volantes* could be the flywheels operating the human machine, i.e. our
      impulses and emotions. In that case the English translation would read: "Oh if only the tacit
      flywheels could be set ...".
19-20. The impact of these lines derives to a large extent from the similarity of sound between
      cintas and *citas* which it is impossible to capture in English.
25.   *humildóse* (arch.), humbled himself.

que no puede caer ni a lloros,
y a cuyo lado ni el Destino pudo entrometer 30
ni un solo dedo suyo.

Así, muerta inmortal.
Así.

LXXIII

Ha triunfado otro ay. La verdad está allí.
Y quien tal actúa ¿no va a saber
amaestrar excelentes digitígrados
para el ratón? ¿Sí ... No ...?

Ha triunfado otro ay y contra nadie. 5
Oh exósmosis de agua químicamente pura.
Ah míos australes. Oh nuestros divinos.
    Tengo, pues, derecho
a estar verde y contento y peligroso, y a ser
el cincel, miedo del bloque basto y vasto; 10
a meter la pata y a la risa.

Absurdo, sólo tú eres puro.
Absurdo, este exceso sólo ante ti se
suda de dorado placer.

which cannot fall even with weeping,
and in whose side not even Destiny could intrude
a single one of its fingers.

Just so, immortal dead one.
Just so.

LXXIII

Another scream has prevailed. That's where the truth is.
And the man who proceeds that way, isn't he going to know
how to train excellent digitigrades
for the mouse? Yes? ... No ...?

Another scream has prevailed and directed against no one.
Oh exosmosis of chemically pure water.
Oh southern mine. Oh divine ours.
        I have the right, then,
to be green and content and dangerous, and to be
the chisel, the terror of the rough, vast block;
and to put my foot in it and to laugh.

Absurd, only you are pure.
Absurd, only in your presence does one sweat
this excess of golden pleasure.

LXXVII

Graniza tanto, como para que yo recuerde
y acreciente las perlas
que he recogido del hocico mismo
de cada tempestad.

No se vaya a secar esta lluvia.   5
A menos que me fuese dado
caer ahora para ella, o que me enterrasen
mojado en el agua
que surtiera de todos los fuegos.

¿Hasta dónde me alcanzará esta lluvia?   10
Temo me quede con algún flanco seco;
temo que ella se vaya, sin haberme probado
en las sequías de increíbles cuerdas vocales,
por las que,
para dar armonía,   15
hay siempre que subir ¡nunca bajar!
¿No subimos acaso para abajo?

Canta, lluvia, en la costa aún sin mar!

LXXVII

It's hailing hard, as if for me to recall
and increase the pearls
I've gathered from the very snout
of every storm.

Don't let this rain go and dry up.
Unless it be granted me
to fall now in its cause, or I were to be buried
steeped in the water
that spouts from all the fires.

How far will this rain reach me?
I'm afraid of being left with some flank still dry;
I'm afraid it'll go, leaving me untried
in the drought of incredible vocal chords,
on which,
to make harmony,
one must always rise, never descend!
Don't we perhaps rise downwards?

Sing, rain, on the coast still without sea!

POEMAS HUMANOS (1939)

absurdity of existence   no order answers

Hasta el día en que vuelva ...

Hasta el día en que vuelva, de esta piedra
nacerá mi talón definitivo,
con su juego de crímenes, su yedra,
su obstinación dramática, su olivo.

Hasta el día en que vuelva, prosiguiendo,   5
con franca rectitud de cojo amargo,
de pozo en pozo, mi periplo, entiendo
que el hombre ha de ser bueno, sin embargo.

Hasta el día en que vuelva y hasta que ande
el animal que soy, entre sus jueces,   10
nuestro bravo meñique será grande,
digno, infinito dedo entre los dedos.

Salutación angélica

Eslavo con respecto a la palmera,
alemán de perfil al sol, inglés sin fin,
francés en cita con los caracoles,
italiano ex profeso, escandinavo de aire,
español de pura bestia, tal el cielo   5
ensartado en la tierra por los vientos,
tal el beso del límite en los hombros.

Mas sólo tú demuestras, descendiendo
o subiendo del pecho, bolchevique,
tus trazos confundibles,   10
tu gesto marital,
tu cara de padre,

HUMAN POEMS (1939)

Till the day I return . . .

Till the day I return, from this stone
will be born my definitive heel,
with its set of crimes, its ivy,
its dramatic obstinacy, its olive tree.

Till the day I return, pursuing,
with the frank rectitude of a bitter cripple,
my peregrination, from well to well, I understand
that man has to be good, nonetheless.

Till the day I return and till the animal
that I am walks among his judges,
our brave pinkie will be great,
honourable, an infinite finger among fingers.

Angelic Greeting

Slav in relation to the palm tree,
German profiled against the sun, Englishman without end,
Frenchman with an appointment with the snails,
Italian expressly so, Scandinavian of air,
Spaniard of pure brutishness, such is heaven
threaded to the earth by the winds,
such is the limit's kiss on the shoulders.

But you alone, Bolshevik, descending
or rising from your breast, display
your confusable features,
your marital gesture,
your fatherly face,

tus piernas de amado,
tu cutis por teléfono,
tu alma perpendicular   15
a la mía,
tus codos de justo
y un pasaporte en blanco en tu sonrisa.

Obrando por el hombre, en nuestras pausas,
matando, tú, a lo largo de tu muerte   20
y a lo ancho de un abrazo salubérrimo,
vi que cuando comías después, tenías gusto,
vi que en tus sustantivos creció yerba.

Yo quisiera, por eso,
tu calor doctrinal, frío y en barras,   25
tu añadida manera de mirarnos
y aquesos tuyos pasos metalúrgicos,
aquesos tuyos pasos de otra vida.

Y digo, bolchevique, tomando esta flaqueza
en su feroz linaje de exhalación terrestre: 30
hijo natural del bien y del mal
y viviendo talvez por vanidad, para que digan,
me dan tus simultáneas estaturas mucha pena,
puesto que tú no ignoras en quién se me hace tarde diariamente,
en quién estoy callado y medio tuerto.   35

your lover's legs,
your complexion by telephone,
your soul perpendicular
to mine,
your just man's elbows
and a blank passport in your smile.

Working as you do for man, during our pauses,
killing as you do your whole death long
and in the spread of a healthy embrace,
I saw that afterwards when you ate you ate with relish,
I saw grass grow in your substantives.

That's why I'd like
your doctrinal heat, cold and in bars,
your added way of looking at us
and those metallurgical steps of yours,
those steps of yours of another life.

And I say, Bolshevik, taking this weakness
in its savage lineage of terrestrial exhalation:
as a natural child of good and evil
and perhaps living out of vanity, so that people will talk,
your simultaneous statures grieve me,
for you can't but know the person within whom I'm kept late every day,
within whom I'm silent and half-blind in one eye.

Epístola a los transeúntes

Reanudo mi día de conejo,
mi noche de elefante en descanso.

Y, entre mí, digo:
ésta es mi inmensidad en bruto, a cántaros,
éste es mi grato peso, que me buscara abajo para pájaro;   5
éste es mi brazo
que por su cuenta rehusó ser ala;
éstas son mis sagradas escrituras,
éstos mis alarmados compañones.

Lúgubre isla me alumbrará continental,   10
mientras el capitolio se apoye en mi íntimo derrumbe
y la asamblea en lanzas clausure mi desfile.

Pero cuando yo muera
de vida y no de tiempo,
cuando lleguen a dos mis dos maletas,   15
éste ha de ser mi estómago en que cupo mi lámpara en pedazos,
ésta aquella cabeza que expió los tormentos del círculo en mis pasos,
éstos esos gusanos que el corazón contó por unidades,
éste ha de ser mi cuerpo solidario
por el que vela el alma individual; éste ha de ser   20
mi hombligo en que maté mis piojos natos,
ésta mi cosa cosa, mi cosa tremebunda.

En tanto, convulsiva, ásperamente
convalece mi freno,
sufriendo como sufro del lenguaje directo del león;   25
y, puesto que he existido entre dos potestades de ladrillo,
convalezco yo mismo sonriendo de mis labios.

---

5.   There is here a play of words involving the colloquial meaning of *pájaro* (penis).

9.   *compañones* is also an archaic variant of *compañeros* (companions). There is a play on the double meaning of the word.

21.   *hombligo* is a misspelling of *ombligo*, perhaps as a play on *hombre* (man).

Epistle to the Passers-by

I resume my rabbit's day,
my night of elephant in repose.

And to myself I say:
This is my immensity in the raw, by the bucketful,
this my pleasurable mass, which sought me below for a bird;
this is my arm
which of its own accord refused to be a wing;
these are my sacred scriptures,
these my aroused testicles.

A lugubrious island will light up my continental way,
while the capitol supports itself on my personal collapse
and the assembly armed with spears brings my parade to a close.

But when I die
of life and not of time,
when my two suitcases amount to two,
this will be my stomach wherein was contained my shattered lamp,
this that head which expiated the torments of walking in a circle,
these those worms that my heart counted one by one,
this will be my solidary body
over which my individual soul keeps watch; this will be
my navel in which I killed my inborn lice,
this my thing of a thing, my tremendous thing.

Meanwhile, convulsively, harshly,
my bridle convalesces,
suffering as I suffer from the direct language of the lion;
and since I've existed between two powers of brick,
I convalesce myself, smiling with my lips.

Los nueve monstruos

Y, desgraciadamente,
el dolor crece en el mundo a cada rato,
crece a treinta minutos por segundo, paso a paso,
y la naturaleza del dolor, es el dolor dos veces
y la condición del martirio, carnívora, voraz,   5
es el dolor dos veces
y la función de la yerba purísima, el dolor
dos veces
y el bien de ser, dolernos doblemente.

Jamás, hombres humanos,   10
hubo tanto dolor en el pecho, en la solapa, en la cartera,
en el vaso, en la carnicería, en la aritmética!
Jamás tanto cariño doloroso,
jamás tan cerca arremetió lo lejos,
jamás el fuego nunca   15
jugó mejor su rol de frío muerto!
Jamás, señor ministro de salud, fue la salud
más mortal
y la migraña extrajo tanta frente de la frente!
Y el mueble tuvo en su cajón, dolor,   20
el corazón, en su cajón, dolor,
la lagartija, en su cajón, dolor.

Crece la desdicha, hermanos hombres,
más pronto que la máquina, a diez máquinas, y crece
con la res de Rousseau, con nuestras barbas;   25
crece el mal por razones que ignoramos
y es una inundación con propios líquidos,
con propio barro y propia nube sólida!
Invierte el sufrimiento posiciones, da función
en que el humor acuoso es vertical   30
al pavimento,
el ojo es visto y esta oreja oída,
y esta oreja da nueve campanadas a la hora
del rayo, y nueve carcajadas

25.   *res* may involve a play on the Latin *res publica* (republic).

The Nine Monsters

And, unfortunately,
pain grows in the world every moment,
grows at thirty minutes a second, step by step,
and the nature of pain is pain twice over
and the condition of martyrdom, carnivorous and voracious,
is pain twice over
and the function of the virgin-pure grass, pain
twice over
and the gift of being, to suffer doubly.

Never, human men,
was there so much pain in the chest, in the lapel, in the wallet,
in the glass, in the butcher's, in arithmetic!
Never so much painful affection,
never did the far-off assail so close,
never did fire ever
play better its role of dead cold!
Never, Mr Minister of Health, was health
more mortal
or did migraine extract so much forehead from the forehead!
Or did the sideboard have pain in its drawer,
the heart pain in its drawer,
the lizard pain in its drawer.

Misfortune grows, brother men,
faster than the engine, at the speed of ten engines, and it grows
with Rousseau's cow, with our beards;
evil grows for reasons we don't know
and it's a flood with its own liquids,
its own mud and its own solid cloud!
Suffering inverts positions, it assigns functions
so that the aqueous humour is vertical
to the pavement,
the eye is seen and this ear heard,
and this ear tolls nine times at the hour
of lightning, gives nine guffaws

a la hora del trigo, y nueve sones hembras 35
a la hora del llanto, y nueve cánticos
a la hora del hambre, y nueve truenos
y nueve látigos, menos un grito.

El dolor nos agarra, hermanos hombres,
por detrás, de perfil, 40
y nos aloca en los cinemas,
nos clava en los gramófonos,
nos desclava en los lechos, cae perpendicularmente
a nuestros boletos, a nuestras cartas;
y es muy grave sufrir, puede uno orar ... 45
Pues de resultas
del dolor, hay algunos
que nacen, otros crecen, otros mueren,
y otros que nacen y no mueren, otros
que sin haber nacido, mueren, y otros 50
que no nacen ni mueren (Son los más).
Y también de resultas
del sufrimiento, estoy triste
hasta la cabeza, y más triste hasta el tobillo,
de ver al pan, crucificado, al nabo, 55
ensangrentado,
llorando, a la cebolla,
al cereal, en general, harina,
a la sal, hecha polvo, al agua, huyendo,
al vino, un ecce-homo, 60
tan pálida a la nieve, al sol tan ardio!
¡Cómo, hermanos humanos,
no deciros que ya no puedo y
ya no puedo con tanto cajón,
tanto minuto, tanta 65
lagartija y tanta
inversión, tanto lejos y tanta sed de sed!
Señor Ministro de Salud: ¿qué hacer?
¡Ah! desgraciadamente, hombres humanos,
hay, hermanos, muchísimo que hacer. 70

---

59.   *hecha polvo* also has the colloquial meaning of "worn out", "shattered".
61.   *ardio = ardido.*

at the hour of wheat, and nine female sounds
at the hour of weeping, and nine canticles
at the hour of hunger, and nine thunderclaps
and nine lashes, minus a shout.

Pain seizes hold of us, brother men,
from behind, in profile,
and it drives us crazy in the cinemas,
nails us on the gramophones,
unnails us in our beds, falls perpendicularly
onto our tickets, onto our letters;
and to suffer is a serious matter, one can always pray . . .
For as a result
of pain, there are some
who are born, others who grow, others who die,
and others who are born and don't die, others
who die unborn, and others
who neither are born or die (They're the majority).
And also as a result
of suffering, I'm sad
up to my head, and sadder down to my ankle,
at seeing bread crucified, the turnip
bloodstained,
the onion weeping,
cereal, in the main, ground to flour,
salt reduced to dust, water fleeing,
wine an ecce-homo,
snow so pale, the sun so burnt-up!
How, brother humans,
not to tell you that I can no longer put up with it and
can no longer put up with so much drawer,
so much minute, so much
lizard and so much
inversion, so much far-off and so much thirst of thirst!
Mr Minister of Health: what's to be done?
Ah, unfortunately, human men,
there is, brothers, so much to be done.

POEMAS HUMANAS

Style - urge to communicate
more exuberant than gloomy ones of Heraldos Negros
optimistic

Me viene, hay días ...

Imp. of paradox
- a didactic device

urge to love is political — marxism is what world needs

Me viene, hay días, una gana ubérrima, política,
de querer, de besar al cariño en sus dos rostros,
y me viene de lejos un querer
demostrativo, otro querer amar, de grado o fuerza,

even if they don't want it (marxism)

al que me odia, al que rasga su papel, al muchachito,   5
a la que llora por el que lloraba,

desire to give

al rey del vino, al esclavo del agua,
al que ocultóse en su ira,
al que suda, al que pasa, al que sacude su persona en mi alma.

al que = 'anaphora' (device)
al que (used in political speeches poetry of person

Y quiero, por lo tanto, acomodarle   10
al que me habla, su trenza; sus cabellos, al soldado;
su luz, al grande; su grandeza, al chico.
Quiero planchar directamente

paradox - (you have to reflect to understand them)

un pañuelo al que no puede llorar
y, cuando estoy triste o me duele la dicha,   15
remendar a los niños y a los genios.

the good are vulnerable in this world?

paradox

Quiero ayudar al bueno a ser su poquillo de malo
y me urge estar sentado   *religious illusion (marxism is an*
a la diestra del zurdo, y responder al mudo,   *alt. to Xianity*
tratando de serle útil en   *+capitalism)*   20
lo que puedo, y también quiero muchísimo   *(to replace other ideals)*

Jesus sat right hand of God in Lord's prayer

lavarle al cojo el pie *Jesus washes feet of poor*
y ayudarle a dormir al tuerto próximo.

¡Ah querer, éste, el mío, éste, el mundial,
interhumano y parroquial, provecto!   25
Me viene a pelo,   *— political urge to love*
desde el cimiento, desde la ingle pública,   *— sexual allusion - he's not*
y, viniendo de lejos, da ganas de besarle   *a typical marxist.*
la bufanda al cantor,
y al que sufre, besarle en su sartén,   30
al sordo, en su rumor craneano, impávido;
al que me da lo que olvidé en mi seno,
en su Dante, en su Chaplin, en sus hombros.

paradox (love, violence)

Quiero, para terminar,
cuando estoy al borde célebre de la violencia, *— frustration at*   35
                                                    imposing his ideas

66

or the role of violence in the marxist rev.
famous revd
past or its well known to us all.
or his own difficulty to 'love' (humanity)

[Handwritten annotations at top: Meter - free verse = abandonment of ... regularity (cf Vallejo as well - not typical / rhyme that is there - stands out. Marxist only)]

[Handwritten: Xian imagery throughout -- succour etc ...]

There comes over me, some days . . .

There comes over me, some days, an exuberant, political urge
to love, to kiss affection on its two cheeks,
and there comes to me from afar a fondness
of a demonstrative kind, a desire to love, willy-nilly,
him who hates me, him who tears up the little boy's paper,
her who weeps for him who wept,
the king of wine, the slave of water,
him who concealed himself in his wrath,
him who sweats, him who passes by, him who shakes his person in my soul.
I want, therefore, to arrange
the tresses of him who talks to me; the soldier's hair;
the great one's light; the little one's greatness.
I want to iron directly
a handkerchief for him who is unable to weep

[Handwritten: 'Love' - a Xian idea not Marxist.]

and, when I'm sad or happiness hurts me,
to mend children and geniuses.

I want to help the good man to be a little bit bad
and I've a pressing urge to be seated
at the right of the left-hander, and to respond to the mute,
trying to be useful to him in
what I can, and I also want very much
to wash the lame man's foot for him
and to help my one-eyed neighbour to sleep.

[Handwritten: Vallejo - a synthesis of X + Marxism (cf interest in LA context]

[Handwritten: parody of Xian discourse!]

Ah love, this love of mine, this universal love,
interhuman and parochial, fully mature!
It comes to me opportunely,
from the foundation, from the public groin,
and, coming from afar, it makes me want to kiss
the singer on his scarf,
and him who suffers, to kiss him on his frying pan,
the deaf man, on his cranial murmur, undaunted;
him who gives me what I forgot in my breast,
on his Dante, on his Chaplin, on his shoulders.

[Handwritten: poem influenced by surrealism (France 20's) (the unconscious)]

I want, finally,
when I'm on the famous verge of violence

67

o lleno de pecho el corazón, querría
ayudar a reír al que sonríe,
ponerle un pajarillo al malvado en plena nuca,
cuidar a los enfermos enfadándolos,
comprarle al vendedor,   40
ayudarle a matar al matador —cosa terrible—
y quisiera yo ser bueno conmigo
en todo.

Sermón sobre la muerte

Y, en fin, pasando luego al dominio de la muerte,
que actúa en escuadrón, previo corchete,
párrafo y llave, mano grande y diéresis,
¿a qué el pupitre asirio? ¿a qué el cristiano púlpito,
el intenso jalón del mueble vándalo   5
o, todavía menos, este esdrújulo retiro?

¿Es para terminar,
mañana, en prototipo del alarde fálico,
en diabetes y en blanca vacinica,
en rostro geométrico, en difunto,   10
que se hacen menester sermón y almendras,
que sobran literalmente patatas
y este espectro fluvial en que arde el oro
y en que se quema el precio de la nieve?
¿Es para eso, que morimos tanto?   15
¿Para sólo morir,
tenemos que morir a cada instante?
¿Y el párrafo que escribo?
¿Y el corchete deísta que enarbolo?
¿Y el escuadrón en que falló mi casco?   20
¿Y la llave que va a todas las puertas?
¿Y la forense diéresis, la mano,
mi patata y mi carne y mi contradicción bajo la sábana?

9.   vacinica = bacinica.

or with my heart full of breast, I'd like
to help him who smiles to laugh,
to place a little bird square on the neck of the evil-doer,
to care for the sick by annoying them,
to buy from the vendor,
to help the killer to kill — a terrible thing —
and I'd like to be good to myself
in everything.

Sermon on Death

And, finally, passing on to the domain of death,
which operates as a squadron, following bracket,
paragraph and key, big hand and dieresis,
to what end the Assyrian desk, to what end the Christian pulpit,
the powerful tug of the Vandal furniture
or, even less, this proparoxytonic retreat?

Is it to end up,
tomorrow, as prototype of phallic strutting,
as diabetes and as white chamber-pot,
as geometric face, as deceased,
that sermons and almonds become necessary,
that literally superfluous are potatoes
and this fluvial spectre in which gold burns
and in which the price of snow is consumed in flames?
Is it for this that we die so often?
Just to die,
must we die every single instant?
And the paragraph I write?
And the deistic bracket I hoist aloft?
And the squadron in which my helmet was found wanting?
And the key which fits all doors?
And the forensic dieresis, the hand,
my potato and my meat and my contradiction under the bedsheet?

¡Loco de mí, lovo de mí, cordero
de mí, sensato, caballísimo de mí!
¡Pupitre, sí, toda la vida; púlpito,
también, toda la muerte!
Sermón de la barbarie: estos papeles;
esdrújulo retiro: este pellejo.

De esta suerte, cogitabundo, aurífero, brazudo,
defenderé mi presa en dos momentos,
con la voz y también con la laringe,
y del olfato físico con que oro
y del instinto de inmovilidad con que ando,
me honraré mientras viva —hay que decirlo;
se enorgullecerán mis moscardones,
porque, al centro, estoy yo, y a la derecha,
también, y a la izquierda, de igual modo.

25

30

35

24.   *lovo = lobo.*

[handwritten: linguistically chaotic mimics chaotic Universe — v. (20th —]

Considerando en frío ...

[handwritten: trying to look at life objectively]
[handwritten: Impartiality ≠ closeness]

[handwritten left margin: words are formula from legal document — like a judgement ✓ is judge]

Considerando en frío, imparcialmente,
que el hombre es triste, tose y, sin embargo, *[handwritten: emotion/physical]*
se complace en su pecho colorado; *[handwritten: man is isolated animal and diseased]*
que lo único que hace es componerse
de días;
que es lóbrego mamífero y se peina ... *[handwritten: 5]*

[handwritten: quite funny?]

Considerando
que el hombre procede suavemente del trabajo
y repercute jefe, suena subordinado; *[handwritten: — objecting to importance of work but 'saavemente']*
que el diagrama del tiempo
es constante diorama en sus medallas *[handwritten: Why i saavemente]*
y, a medio abrir, sus ojos estudiaron, *[handwritten: why suena.]*
desde lejanos tiempos,
su fórmula famélica de masa ...

10

Comprendiendo sin esfuerzo
que el hombre se queda, a veces, pensando,

15

[handwritten: Mysterious in detail but overall message clear]

Mad that I am, wolf that I am, lamb
that I am, sensible, horse through and through that I am!
Desk, yes, all my life; pulpit,
too, all my death!
Sermon of barbarism: these papers;
proparoxytonic retreat: this skin.

In this way, cogitative, auriferous, strong-armed,
I'll defend my prey in two stages,
with my voice and also with my larynx,
and on the physical sense of smell with which I pray
and on the instinct of immobility with which I walk,
I'll pride myself as long as I live — it has to be said;
my hornets will swell with pride,
because there I am in the centre, and on the right,
too, and on the left, likewise.

Considering coldly . . .

*under com- influence at this time
but wouldn't harness poetry to politics*

Considering coldly, impartially,
that man is sad, coughs and, yet,
takes satisfaction in his reddened chest;
that all he does is make himself up
of days;
that he's a gloomy mammal and combs his hair . . .

animal images

gorilla/man

Considering
that man proceeds smoothly from work
and reverberates boss, resounds subordinate;
that the diagram of time
is a constant diorama on his medals
and that, half-open, his eyes have studied,
since distant times,
his famished mass formula . . .

— apathetic man

—sliding to death (time)

achievements

model of a few figures (like as/age)

Understanding without effort
that man at times falls to thinking,

71

como queriendo llorar,
y, sujeto a tenderse como objeto,
se hace buen carpintero, suda, mata
y luego canta, almuerza, se abotona ...   20

Considerando también
que el hombre es en verdad un animal
y, no obstante, al voltear, me da con su tristeza en la cabeza ...

Examinando, en fin,
sus encontradas piezas, su retrete,   25
su desesperación, al terminar su día atroz, borrándolo ...

Comprendiendo
que él sabe que le quiero,
que le odio con afecto y me es, en suma, indiferente ...

Considerando sus documentos generales   30
y mirando con lentes aquel certificado
que prueba que nació muy pequeñito ...

le hago una seña,
viene,
y le doy un abrazo, emocionado.   35
¡Qué más da! Emocionado ... Emocionado ...

Parado en una piedra ...

Parado en una piedra,
desocupado,
astroso, espeluznante,
a la orilla del Sena, va y viene.
Del río brota entonces la conciencia,   5
con peciolo y rasguños de árbol ávido:
del río sube y baja la ciudad, hecha de lobos abrazados.

El parado la ve yendo y viniendo,
monumental, llevando sus ayunos en la cabeza cóncava,

as though wanting to weep,
and that, subject to being laid out like an object,
he becomes a good carpenter, sweats, kills
and then sings, eats lunch, buttons himself up . . .

[handwritten: hiding from meaninglessness in activity]

Considering also
that man is truly an animal
and yet, when he turns round, he bashes me on the head with his sadness . . .

[handwritten: Summary of 3 previous verses]

Examining, finally,
his discordant parts, his lavatory,
his despair on finishing his atrocious day, erasing it . . .

[handwritten: body/machine — specimen — animal functions; he touches poet, becomes a person now as √ more reconciled to mankind]

Understanding
that he knows I love him,
that I hate him with affection and he is, in short, a matter of indifference to me . . .

[handwritten: paradoxes]

Considering his general documents
and scrutinising with spectacles that certificate
which proves he was born very tiny . . .

[handwritten: scientist/judge researcher — √ is an outsider but has feelings]

I signal to him,
he comes over,
and I give him a hug, moved.
So what! Moved . . . Moved . . .

[handwritten: human touch can overcome emptiness of life. embarrassed admission]

Idle on a stone . . .

Idle on a stone,
out of work,
shabby, horrifying,
on the banks of the Seine he comes and goes.
From the river sprouts consciousness then,
with petiole and scratches of an avid tree:
from the river the city rises and falls, made up of embracing wolves.

The jobless man watches it coming and going,
monumental, carrying his fasts in his concave head,

en el pecho sus piojos purísimos 10
y abajo
su pequeño sonido, el de su pelvis,
callado entre dos grandes decisiones,
y abajo,
más abajo, 15
un papelito, un clavo, una cerilla ...

¡Éste es, trabajadores, aquel
que en la labor sudaba para afuera,
que suda hoy para adentro su secreción de sangre rehusada!
Fundidor del cañón, que sabe cuántas zarpas son acero, 20
tejedor que conoce los hilos positivos de sus venas,
albañil de pirámides,
constructor de descensos por columnas
serenas, por fracasos triunfales,
parado individual entre treinta millones de parados, 25
andante en multitud,
¡qué salto el retratado en su talón
y qué humo el de su boca ayuna, y cómo
su talle incide, canto a canto, en su herramienta atroz, parada,
y qué idea de dolorosa válvula en su pómulo! 30

También parado el hierro frente al horno,
paradas las semillas con sus sumisas síntesis al aire,
parados los petróleos conexos,
parada en sus auténticos apóstrofes la luz,
parados de crecer los laureles, 35
paradas en un pie las aguas móviles
y hasta la tierra misma, parada de estupor ante este paro,
¡qué salto el retratado en sus tendones!
¡qué transmisión entablan sus cien pasos!
¡cómo chilla el motor en su tobillo! 40
¡cómo gruñe el reloj, paseándose impaciente a sus espaldas!
¡cómo oye deglutir a los patrones
el trago que le falta, camaradas,
y el pan que se equivoca de saliva,
y, oyéndolo, sintiéndolo, en plural, humanamente, 45
cómo clava el relámpago
su fuerza sin cabeza en su cabeza!
y lo que hacen, abajo, entonces, ¡ay!

in his chest his purest lice
and below
his little noise, that of his pelvis,
hushed between two great decisions,
and below,
further down,
a scrap of paper, a nail, a match . . .

This, workers, is the man
who in his labour used to sweat outwards,
who today sweats inwards his secretion of blood rejected!
The founder of the cannon, who knows how many claws make steel,
the weaver who knows the positive threads of his veins,
the mason of pyramids,
the builder of descents by serene
columns, by triumphant failures,
one jobless individual among thirty million jobless,
walking amid a multitude,
what a leap that depicted in his heel
and what smoke that from his fasting mouth, and how
his physique slots, edge to edge, into his atrocious, idle tool,
and what a notion of painful valve in his cheekbone!

At a standstill, too, the iron before the furnace,
at a standstill the seeds with their submissive syntheses in the air,
at a standstill the connected petroleums,
at a standstill the light in its authentic apostrophes,
at a standstill the laurels, stopped in their growth,
at a standstill on one foot the mobile waters
and even the earth itself at a stupefied standstill in face of this standstill.
What a leap that depicted in his tendons!
What transmission started up by his hundred steps!
How the engine shrieks in his ankle!
How the clock growls, walking impatiently up and down at his back!
How he hears the bosses guzzle
the drink that he lacks, comrades,
and the bread that chooses the wrong saliva,
and hearing it, experiencing it, in the plural, humanly,
how lightning nails
its headless force into his head!
And you should see what they're doing then down below, alas,

más abajo, camaradas,
el papelucho, el clavo, la cerilla,   50
el pequeño sonido, el piojo padre!

Va corriendo, andando ...

Va corriendo, andando, huyendo
de sus pies ...
Va con dos nubes en su nube,
sentado apócrifo, en la mano insertos
sus tristes paras, sus entonces fúnebres.   5

Corre de todo, andando
entre protestas incoloras; huye
subiendo, huye
bajando, huye
a paso de sotana, huye   10
alzando al mal en brazos,
huye
directamente a sollozar a solas.

Adonde vaya,
lejos de sus fragosos, cáusticos talones,   15
lejos del aire, lejos de su viaje,
a fin de huir, huir y huir y huir
de sus pies —hombre en dos pies, parado
de tanto huir— habrá sed de correr.

¡Y ni el árbol, si endosa hierro de oro!   20
¡Y ni el hierro, si cubre su hojarasca!
Nada, sino sus pies,
nada sino su breve calofrío,
sus paras vivos, sus entonces vivos ...

---

5.   Alternatively, *paras* could be translated as "fors" or "in-order-tos" and *entonces* as "thens".

further down, comrades,
that miserable scrap of paper, the nail, the match,
the little noise, the father louse!

He goes running, walking . . .

He goes running, walking, fleeing
from his feet . . .
He goes with two clouds in his cloud,
an apocryphal sitter, holding inserted in his hand
his sad wherefores, his mournful therefores.

He runs from everything, moving
between colourless protests; he flees
climbing, he flees
descending, he flees
at cassock's pace, he flees
bearing evil in his arms,
he flees
in a straight line to weep alone.

Wherever he goes,
far from his rough, caustic heels,
far from the air, far from his journey,
in order to flee, flee and flee and flee
from his feet — man on two feet, at a halt
from so much fleeing — there'll be a thirst for running.

And not even the tree, if he coats iron with gold!
And not even the iron, if he covers up its dead foliage!
Nothing but his feet,
nothing but his brief shudder,
his living wherefores, his living therefores . . .

Piedra negra sobre una piedra blanca

Me moriré en París con aguacero,
un día del cual tengo ya el recuerdo.
Me moriré en París —y no me corro—
talvez un jueves, como es hoy, de otoño.

Jueves será, porque hoy, jueves, que proso   5
estos versos, los húmeros me he puesto
a la mala y, jamás como hoy, me he vuelto,
con todo mi camino, a verme solo.

César Vallejo ha muerto, le pegaban
todos sin que él les haga nada;   10
le daban duro con un palo y duro

también con una soga; son testigos
los días jueves y los huesos húmeros,
la soledad, la lluvia, los caminos . . .

_____

7.   _a la mala_ (Per.) = _por la mala, de mala gana._

78

Black Stone on a White Stone

I'll die in Paris when it's raining hard
on a day that's already lodged in my memory.
I'll die in Paris — and I'm not running away —
maybe some Thursday, like today, in autumn.

Thursday it'll be, for today, Thursday, when I prose
these verses, I've donned my humeri
with reluctance and never as today,
for all my long road, have I ever seen myself so alone.

César Vallejo is dead, they all beat him
when he'd done nothing to them;
they hit him hard with a stick and hard

too with a rope; witnesses are
the Thursdays and the humerus bones,
the loneliness, the rain, the roads . . .

Intensidad y altura

Quiero escribir, pero me sale espuma,
quiero decir muchísimo y me atollo;
no hay cifra hablada que no sea suma,
no hay pirámide escrita, sin cogollo.

Quiero escribir, pero me siento puma;   5
quiero laurearme, pero me encebollo.
No hay toz hablada, que no llegue a bruma,
no hay dios ni hijo de dios, sin desarrollo.

Vámonos, pues, por eso, a comer yerba,
carne de llanto, fruta de gemido,   10
nuestra alma melancólica en conserva.

Vámonos! Vámonos! Estoy herido;
vámonos a beber lo ya bebido,
vámonos, cuervo, a fecundar tu cuerva.

6.   Given that *encebollar* means "to season with onion" and that an *encebollado* is an onion
stew, *encebollarse* would seem to mean "to make a stew of oneself".
7.   *toz* is a neologism conflating *voz* (word, voice) and *tos* (cough).

Intensity and Height

I want to write, but out comes foam,
I want to say so much and get bogged down;
there's no spoken cipher that isn't a sum,
there's no written pyramid without a core.

I want to write, but I feel I'm a puma;
I want to crown myself with laurels, but I stew in onion.
There's no spoken splutterance that doesn't end in mist,
there's no god nor son of god without development.

So let's go, then, and feed on grass,
flesh of lamentation, fruit of wailing,
our melancholy soul preserved in pickle.

Let's go! Let's go! I'm sorely wounded;
let's go drink what's already drunk,
let's go, crow, and impregnate your mate.

Un pilar soportando consuelos ...

Un pilar soportando consuelos,
pilar otro,
pilar en duplicado, pilaroso
y como nieto de una puerta oscura.
Ruido perdido, el uno, oyendo, al borde del cansancio;   5
bebiendo, el otro, dos a dos, con asas.

¿Ignoro acaso el año de este día,
el odio de este amor, las tablas de esta frente?
¿Ignoro que esta tarde cuesta días?
¿Ignoro que jamás se dice "nunca", de rodillas?   10

Los pilares que vi me están oyendo;
otros pilares son, doses y nietos tristes de mi pierna.
¡Lo digo en cobre americano,
que le bebe a la plata tanto fuego!

Consolado en terceras nupcias,   15
pálido, nacido,
voy a cerrar mi pila bautismal, esta vidriera,
este susto con tetas,
este dedo en capilla,
corazónmente unido a mi esqueleto.   20

8.   I have chosen to interpret *tablas* as mathematical tables, but alternatively it could mean "planks".

13-14. These lines seem to be an elaboration of the expression *hablar en plata* (to speak bluntly). The sense would seem to be: "I state it with American bluntness."

20.   *corazónmente* is not only an adverbial form of the noun, but conjoins *corazón* (heart) and *mente* (mind).

A pillar supporting solace . . .

A pillar supporting solace,
another pillar,
pillar in duplicate, pillarish
and like the grandchild of a dark door.
Wasted noise, the one, listening on the edge of exhaustion;
drinking, the other, two gulps at a time, with handles.

Don't I know, perhaps, the year of this day,
the hatred of this love, the tables of this forehead?
Don't I know that this evening costs days?
Don't I know that one never says "never" on one's knees?

The pillars I saw are listening to me;
other pillars they are, sad twos and grandchildren of my leg.
I say it in American copper,
which from silver absorbs so much fire!

Consoled in third nuptials,
pallid, born,
I'm going to close my baptismal font, this showcase,
this terror with teats,
this finger in the death cell,
heartily united to my skeleton.

La rueda del hambriento

Por entre mis propios dientes salgo humeando,
dando voces, pujando,
bajándome los pantalones . . .
Vaca mi estómago, vaca mi yeyuno,
la miseria me saca por entre mis propios dientes,   5
cogido con un palito por el puño de la camisa.

Una piedra en que sentarme
¿no habrá ahora para mí?
Aun aquella piedra en que tropieza la mujer que ha dado a luz,
la madre del cordero, la causa, la raíz,   10
¿ésa no habrá ahora para mí?
¡Siquiera aquella otra,
que ha pasado agachándose por mi alma!
Siquiera
la calcárida o la mala (humilde océano)   15
o la que ya no sirve ni para ser tirada contra el hombre,
¡ésa dádmela ahora para mí!

Siquiera la que hallaren atravesada y sola en un insulto,
¡ésa dádmela ahora para mí!
Siquiera la torcida y coronada, en que resuena   20
solamente una vez el andar de las rectas conciencias,
o, al menos, esa otra, que arrojada en digna curva,
va a caer por sí misma,
en profesión de entraña verdadera,
¡ésa dádmela ahora para mí!   25

Un pedazo de pan, ¿tampoco habrá ahora para mí?
Ya no más he de ser lo que siempre he de ser,
pero dadme
una piedra en que sentarme,
pero dadme,   30
por favor, un pedazo de pan en que sentarme,
pero dadme
en español
algo, en fin, de beber, de comer, de vivir, de reposarse,

15.   *calcárido* would seem to be a neologism conflating *calcáreo* (calcareous) and *árido* (arid).

The Starving Man's Wheel

Out between my own teeth I come steaming,
yelling, straining,
dropping my trousers . . .
My stomach's out of work, my jejunum's out of work,
destitution pulls me out between my own teeth,
caught on a toothpick by the cuff of my shirt.

A stone to sit down on,
isn't there that for me any more?
Even that stone tripped over by the woman who's given birth,
the mother of the lamb, the cause, the root,
isn't there that for me any more?
At the very least that other one
that's gone cowering through my soul!
At the very least
the calcarid one or the bad one (humble ocean)
or the one that's useless now even for throwing at man,
give me that one now for myself!

Even the one found askew and alone in an insult,
give me that one now for myself!
Even the twisted and crowned one, in which there echoes
only once the tread of upright consciences,
or, at least, that other one which, thrown in dignified curve,
will fall by itself,
in profession of true entrail,
give me that one now for myself!

A piece of bread, isn't there that for me now either?
From now on I'm just to be what I'm always to be,
but give me
a stone to sit down on,
but give me,
please, a piece of bread to sit down on,
but give me
in Spanish
something, in short, to drink, to eat, to live, to rest,

y después me iré . . .   35
Hallo una extraña forma, está muy rota
y sucia mi camisa
y ya no tengo nada, esto es horrendo.

¡Y si después de tantas palabras . . . !

¡Y si después de tantas palabras,
no sobrevive la palabra!
¡Si después de las alas de los pájaros,
no sobrevive el pájaro parado!
¡Más valdría, en verdad,   5
que se lo coman todo y acabemos!

¡Haber nacido para vivir de nuestra muerte!
¡Levantarse del cielo hacia la tierra
por sus propios desastres
y espiar el momento de apagar con su sombra su tiniebla!   10
¡Más valdría, francamente,
que se lo coman todo y qué más da! . . .

¡Y si después de tanta historia, sucumbimos,
no ya de eternidad,
sino de esas cosas sencillas, como estar   15
en la casa o ponerse a cavilar!
¡Y si luego encontramos,
de buenas a primeras, que vivimos,
a juzgar por la altura de los astros,
por el peine y las manchas del pañuelo!   20
¡Más valdría, en verdad,
que se lo coman todo, desde luego!

Se dirá que tenemos
en uno de los ojos much pena
y también en el otro, much pena   25
y en los dos, cuando miran, much pena . . .
Entonces . . . ¡Claro! . . . Entonces . . . ¡ni palabra!

13.   There may be a play on the double meaning of *historia* (history/story, tale).

and then I'll go away ...
I notice a strange shape, my shirt's
all torn and filthy
and I've nothing left, this is horrendous.

And if after so many words ...!

And if after so many words,
the word doesn't survive!
If after the wings of the birds,
the resting bird doesn't survive!
It would be better, it truly would,
if it were all gobbled up and we had an end to it!

To have been born to live off our death!
To lift ourselves from the heavens to the earth
by our own disasters
and to keep watch for the moment when we extinguish our darkness with our shadow!
It would be better, frankly,
if it were all gobbled up and what does it matter! ...

And if after so much history, we succumb,
not now to eternity,
but to those simple little things, like being
at home or setting oneself to brooding!
And if then we discover,
all of a sudden, that we live,
judging from the height of the stars,
by the comb and the stains on the handkerchief!
It would be better, it truly would,
if it were all gobbled up, that's for sure!

They'll say that we've
a lot of sadness in one of our eyes
and a lot of sadness in the other as well
and a lot of sadness in both of them, when they stare ...
Well, then ... Of course!... Well, then ... not another word!

París, octubre 1936

De todo esto yo soy el único que parte.
De este banco me voy, de mis calzones,
de mi gran situación, de mis acciones,
de mi número hendido parte a parte,
de todo esto yo soy el único que parte.   5

De los Campos Elíseos o al dar vuelta
la extraña callejuela de la Luna,
mi defunción se va, parte mi cuna,
y, rodeada de gente, sola, suelta,
mi semejanza humana dase vuelta   10
y despacha sus sombras una a una.

Y me alejo de todo, porque todo
se queda para hacer la coartada:
mi zapato, su ojal, también su lodo
y hasta el doblez del codo   15
de mi propia camisa abotonada.

2-3.   There is a play on the double sense of *banco* (bench/bank) and *acciones* (actions/shares). In the second case I have tried to capture some of the ambiguity by translating *acciones* as "deeds". In the first case, however, the play on words is impossible to convey in English.

Los desgraciados

Ya va a venir el día; da
cuerda a tu brazo, búscate debajo
del colchón, vuelve a pararte
en tu cabeza, para andar derecho.
Ya va a venir el día, ponte el saco.   5

Ya va a venir el día; ten
fuerte en la mano a tu intestino grande, reflexiona,
antes de meditar, pues es horrible
cuando le cae a uno la desgracia
y se le cae a uno a fondo el diente.   10

Paris, October 1936

From all this I'm the only one leaving.
From this bench I'm going, from my trousers,
from my grand position, from my deeds,
from my number split down the middle,
from all this I'm the only one leaving.

From the Elysian Fields or the bend
of the strange alley of the Moon,
my demise goes off, my cradle departs,
and surrounded by people, alone, unattached,
my human semblance turns around
and dispatches its shadows one by one.

And I'm leaving it all behind, because it's all
remaining here to serve as alibi:
my shoe, its lacehole, its mud as well,
and even the crease in the elbow
of my own buttoned shirt.

The Wretched

The day is about to come; wind up
your arm, look for yourself under
the mattress, stand up again
in your head, to walk erect.
The day is about to come, put on your jacket.

The day is about to come; hold
your large intestine firmly in your hand, reflect
before you meditate, for it's horrible
when misfortune falls on one
and one's tooth falls out, right down into one.

Necesitas comer, pero, me digo,
no tengas pena, que no es de pobres
la pena, el sollozar junto a su tumba;
remiéndate, recuerda,
confía en tu hilo blanco, fuma, pasa lista   15
a tu cadena y guárdala detrás de tu retrato.
Ya va a venir el día, ponte el alma.

Ya va a venir el día; pasan,
han abierto en el hotel un ojo,
azotándolo, dándole con un espejo tuyo ...   20
¿Tiemblas? Es el estado remoto de la frente
y la nación reciente del estómago.
Roncan aún ... ¡Qué universo se lleva este ronquido!
¡Cómo quedan tus poros, enjuiciándolo!
¡Con cuántos doses, ¡ay! estás tan solo!   25
Ya va a venir el día, ponte el sueño.

Ya va a venir el día, repito
por el órgano oral de tu silencio
y urge tomar la izquierda con el hambre
y tomar la derecha con la sed; de todos modos,   30
absténte de ser pobre con los ricos,
atiza
tu frío, porque en él se integra mi calor, amada víctima.
Ya va a venir el día, ponte el cuerpo.

Ya va a venir el día;   35
la mañana, la mar, el meteoro, van
en pos de tu cansancio, con banderas,
y, por tu orgullo clásico, las hienas
cuentan sus pasos al compás del asno,
la panadera piensa en ti,   40
el carnicero piensa en ti, palpando
el hacha en que están presos
el acero y el hierro y el metal; jamás olvides
que durante la misa no hay amigos.
Ya va a venir el día, ponte el sol.   45

Ya viene el día; dobla
el aliento, triplica

You need to eat, but, I tell myself,
don't feel sorry for yourself, for it isn't for the poor
is sorrow, that sobbing by one's graveside;
patch yourself up, remember,
trust in your white thread, have a smoke, run a check
over your chain and stash it behind your portrait.
The day is about to come, put on your soul.

The day is about to come; people go past,
in the hotel they've opened an eye,
lashing it, beating it with a mirror of yours . . .
You're trembling? It's the remote state of the forehead
and the recent nation of the stomach.
They're still snoring . . . What a universe is borne away by that snore!
What a state your pores are in, passing judgement on it!
Despite all those twos, alas, how alone you are!
The day is about to come, put on your dream.

The day is about to come, I repeat
through the oral organ of your silence
and it's imperative that you go left with your hunger
and go right with your thirst; in all events,
abstain from being poor with the rich,
poke up
your cold, for in it my warmth is constituted, beloved victim.
The day is about to come, put on your body.

The day is about to come;
the morning, the sea, the meteor follow
behind your weariness, with banners,
and because of your classic pride, the hyenas
measure their tread to the rhythm of the donkey,
the baker's wife is thinking of you,
the butcher is thinking of you, fondling
the cleaver in which are imprisoned
steel and iron and metal; never forget
that during Mass there are no friends.
The day is about to come, put on the sun.

The day is coming now; double
your spirits, triple

tu bondad rencorosa
y da codos al miedo, nexo y énfasis,
pues tú, como se observa en tu entrepierna y siendo   50
el malo ¡ay! inmortal,
has soñado esta noche que vivías
de nada y morías de todo . . .

El acento me pende . . .

El acento me pende del zapato;
le oigo perfectamente
sucumbir, lucir, doblarse en forma de ámbar
y colgar, colorante, mala sombra.
Me sobra así el tamaño,   5
me ven jueces desde un árbol,
me ven con sus espaldas ir de frente,
entrar a mi martillo,
pararme a ver a una niña
y, al pie de un urinario, alzar los hombros.   10

Seguramente nadie está a mi lado,
me importa poco, no lo necesito;
seguramente han dicho que me vaya:
lo siento claramente.

¡Cruelísimo tamaño el de rezar!   15
¡Humillación, fulgor, profunda selva!
Me sobra ya tamaño, bruma elástica,
rapidez por encima y desde y junto.
¡Imperturbable! ¡Imperturbable! Suenan
luego, después, fatídicos teléfonos.   20
Es el acento: es él.

your resentful good nature
and elbow away fear, nexus and emphasis,
for, as can be seen in your crotch and it being the case,
alas, that the man of evil is immortal,
you dreamt this night that you were living
on nothing and you were dying of everything . . .

The accent dangles . . .

The accent dangles from my shoe;
I hear it perfectly
as it succumbs, shines, doubles over in the form of amber
and hangs there, casting colour, an evil shadow.
This way my stature's too much for me,
judges watch me from a tree,
with their backs they watch me go forward,
run into my hammer,
stop to look at a girl
and shrug my shoulders in front of a urinal.

It's a certainty no one's at my side,
I don't much care, I don't need anyone;
it's a certainty they've told me to go away:
I can sense it quite clearly.

Cruelest of statures that of praying!
Humiliation, brilliance, deep forest!
It's too much for me now, my stature, elastic mist,
speed above and from and alongside.
Imperturbable! Imperturbable! There ring
next, afterwards, ominous telephones.
It's the accent: it's it.

Quiere y no quiere . . .

Quiere y no quiere su color mi pecho,
por cuyas bruscas vías voy, lloro con palo,
trato de ser feliz, lloro en mi mano,
recuerdo, escribo
y remacho una lágrima en mi pómulo.   5

Quiere su rojo el mal, el bien su rojo enrojecido
por el hacha suspensa,
por el trote del ala a pie volando,
y no quiere y sensiblemente
no quiere aquesto el hombre;   10
no quiere estar en su alma
acostado, en la sien latidos de asta,
el bimano, el muy bruto, el muy filósofo.

Así, casi no soy, me vengo abajo
desde el arado en que socorro a mi alma   15
y casi, en proporción, casi enaltézcome.
Que saber por qué tiene la vida este perrazo,
por qué lloro, por qué,
cejón, inhábil, veleidoso, hube nacido
gritando;   20
saberlo, comprenderlo
al son de un alfabeto competente,
sería padecer por un ingrato.

¡Y no! ¡No! ¡No! ¡Qué ardid, ni paramento!
Congoja, sí, con sí firme y frenético,   25
coriáceo, rapaz, quiere y no quiere, cielo y pájaro;
congoja, sí, con toda la bragueta.
Contienda entre dos llantos, robo de una sola ventura,
vía indolora en que padezco en chanclos
de la velocidad de andar a ciegas.   30

---

24.   *ardid* is here used in its archaic sense of "feat", "act of prowess".

It wants and doesn't want . . .

It wants and doesn't want its colour, does my chest,
along whose brusque tracks I go, weeping with a stick,
trying to be happy, weeping into my hand,
remembering, writing
and riveting a tear onto my cheekbone.

Evil wants its red, good its red reddened
by the poised axe,
by the trot of the wing flying on foot,
and man doesn't want, palpably
doesn't want that;
he doesn't want to lie abed
in his soul, with the throbbing of horns in his temple,
bimane that he is, the great brute, the great philosopher.

Thus, I almost am not, I come tumbling down
from the plough in which I succour my soul
and almost, in proportion, almost raise myself up.
For to know why life is such a bitch,
why I weep, why,
heavy-browed, awkward, unreliable, I was born
screaming;
to know it, to understand it
after the fashion of a competent alphabet,
would be to suffer from being an ingrate.

And no! No! No! What prowess or frills?
Anguish, yes, with a yes firm and frantic,
coriaceous, rapacious, wants and doesn't want, sky and bird;
anguish, yes, with the whole of one's fly.
A contest between two lamentations, theft of a one and only bliss,
painless road on which I suffer in clogs
the speed of journeying blind.

El alma que sufrió de ser su cuerpo

Tú sufres de una glándula endocrínica, se ve,
o, quizá,
sufres de mí, de mi sagacidad escueta, tácita.
Tú padeces del diáfano antropoide, allá, cerca,
donde está la tiniebla tenebrosa.   5
Tú das vuelta al sol, agarrándote el alma,
extendiendo tus juanes corporales
y ajustándote el cuello; eso se ve.
Tú sabes lo que te duele,
lo que te salta al anca,   10
lo que baja por ti con soga al suelo.
Tú, pobre hombre, vives; no lo niegues,
si mueres; no lo niegues,
si mueres de tu edad ¡ay! y de tu época.
Y, aunque llores, bebes,   15
y, aunque sangres, alimentas a tu híbrido colmillo,
a tu vela tristona y a tus partes.
Tú sufres, tú padeces y tú vuelves a sufrir horriblemente,
desgraciado mono,
jovencito de Darwin,   20
alguacil que me atisbas, atrocísimo microbio.
Y tú lo sabes a tal punto,
que lo ignoras, soltándote a llorar.
Tú, luego, has nacido; eso
también se ve de lejos, infeliz y cállate,   25
y soportas la calle que te dio la suerte
y a tu ombligo interrogas: ¿dónde? ¿cómo?

Amigo mío, estás completamente,
hasta el pelo, en el año treinta y ocho,
nicolás o santiago, tal o cual,   30
estés contigo o con tu aborto o con-
migo,
y cautivo en tu enorme libertad,

---

7.   *juanes corporales*: literally, "corporal johns". The phrase alludes to *juanetes* (prominent
      knuckle-bones on the foot, bunions), so called because they were regarded as a sign of a
      country bumpkin (*Juan*).

96

The Soul that Suffered from Being its Body

You're suffering from an endocrine gland, that's obvious,
or, perhaps,
it's me you're suffering from, from my stark, tacit sagacity.
You're suffering from the diaphanous anthropoid, there, close by,
where lies dark darkness.
You circle the sun, clutching your soul,
stretching out your bunions
and straightening your collar; that's obvious.
You know what's hurting you,
what leaps on to your hind-quarters,
what descends down you with a rope to the ground.
Poor man, you're alive: don't deny it,
since you're dying; don't deny it,
since you're dying of your age, alas!, and of your epoch.
And even if you weep, you drink,
and even if you bleed, you feed your hybrid fang,
your gloomy candle and your parts.
You suffer, you endure and you suffer again horribly,
miserable ape,
Darwin's young lad,
constable with an eye on me, most atrocious of microbes.
And you know it to the point
where you don't know it, bursting into tears.
You've been born, then; that
too can be seen a mile off, poor wretch and shut up,
and you endure the street chance gave you
and you question your navel: where? how?

Friend, you're wholly and completely,
right up to your hair, in the year thirty-eight,
nicholas or james or what's-your-name,
whether you're with yourself or with your abortion or with
me,
and captive in your enormous freedom,

---

11.   *por ti* could equally mean "because of you".

arrastrado por tu hércules autónomo . . .
Pero si tú calculas en tus dedos hasta dos,   35
es peor; no lo niegues, hermanito.

¿Que no? ¿Que sí, pero que no?
¡Pobre mono! . . . ¡Dame la pata! . . . No. La mano, he dicho.
¡Salud! ¡Y sufre!

Al revés de las aves . . .

Al revés de las aves del monte,
que viven del valle,
aquí, una tarde,
aquí, presa, metaloso, terminante,
vino el Sincero con sus nietos pérfidos,   5
y nosotros quedámonos, que no hay
más madera en la cruz de la derecha,
ni más hierro en el clavo de la izquierda,
que un apretón de manos entre zurdos.

Vino el Sincero, ciego, con sus lámparas.   10
Se vio al Pálido, aquí, bastar
al Encarnado;
nació de puro humilde el Grande;
la guerra,
esta tórtola mía, nunca nuestra,   15
diseñóse, borróse, ovó, matáronla.

Llevóse el Ebrio al labio un roble, porque
amaba, y una astilla
de roble, porque odiaba;
trenzáronse las trenzas de los potros   20
y la crin de las potencias;
cantaron los obreros; fui dichoso.

---

4.   *metaloso* is a neologism formed from *metal*.

dragged along by your autonomous hercules ...
But if you count on your fingers up to two,
it's worse; don't deny it, kid.

No? Yes but no?
Poor ape! ... Give me your paw! ... Your hand, I mean.
Good health! And keep suffering!

Contrary to the birds ...

Contrary to the birds of the mountain,
which live off the valley,
here, one afternoon,
here, a prey, metallous, categorical,
came the Sincere One with his perfidious grandchildren,
and we remained, for there's
no more wood in the cross on the right
nor more iron in the nail on the left
than a handshake between left-handers.

The Sincere One came, blind, with his lamps.
The Pale One was here seen to suffice
for the Ruddy;
the Great One was born of sheer humbleness;
war,
that turtle-dove of mine, never ours,
sketched itself, erased itself, laid eggs, was killed.

The Inebriate raised an oak to his lip, because
he loved, and a splinter
of oak, because he hated;
plaited were the tresses of the colts
and the manes of the powers;
the workers sang; I was happy.

El Pálido abrazóse al Encarnado
y el Ebrio saludónos, escondiéndose.
Como era aquí y al terminar el día,   25
¡qué más tiempo que aquella plazoleta!
¡qué año mejor que esa gente!
¡qué momento más fuerte que ese siglo!

Pues de lo que hablo no es
sino de lo que pasa en esta época, y   30
de lo que ocurre en China y en España, y en el mundo.
(Walt Whitman tenía un pecho suavísimo y respiraba y nadie
sabe lo que él hacía cuando lloraba en su comedor.)

Pero, volviendo a lo nuestro
y al verso que decía, fuera entonces   35
que vi que el hombre es malnacido,
mal vivo, mal muerto, mal moribundo,
y, naturalmente,
el tartufo sincero desespérase,
el pálido (es el pálido de siempre)   40
será pálido por algo,
y el ebrio, entre la sangre humana y la leche animal,
abátese, da, y opta por marcharse.

Todo esto
agítase, ahora mismo,   45
en mi vientre de macho extrañamente.

The Pale One embraced the Ruddy
and the Inebriate greeted us, hiding himself.
Since it was here and at the end of the day,
what time more than that little square!
what year better than those folk!
what moment intenser than that century!

For what I'm talking about is
nothing other than what's taking place in these times, and
what's happening in China and in Spain and in the world.
(Walt Whitman had the softest of breasts and breathed and no one
knows what he was doing when he wept in his dining-room.)

But getting back to our subject
and to the verse I was saying, it was then
that I saw that man is ill-born,
ill-living, ill-dead, ill-dying,
and, naturally,
the sincere tartuffe despairs,
the pale one (he's the same old pale one as ever)
must be pale for a reason,
and the inebriate, between human blood and animal milk,
loses heart, gives up and opts to walk away.

All this
churns over queerly,
right now, here in my male's belly.

Ello es que . . .

Ello es que el lugar donde me pongo
el pantalón, es una casa donde
me quito la camisa en alta voz
y donde tengo un suelo, un alma, un mapa de mi España.
Ahora mismo hablaba   5
de mí conmigo, y ponía
sobre un pequeño libro un pan tremendo
y he, luego, hecho el traslado, he trasladado,
queriendo canturrear un poco, el lado
derecho de la vida al lado izquierdo;   10
más tarde, me he lavado todo, el vientre,
briosa, dignamente;
he dado vuelta a ver lo que se ensucia,
he raspado lo que me lleva tan cerca
y he ordenado bien el mapa que   15
cabeceaba o lloraba, no lo sé.

Mi casa, por desgracia, es una casa,
un suelo por ventura, donde vive
con su inscripción mi cucharita amada,
mi querido esqueleto ya sin letras,   20
la navaja, un cigarro permanente.
De veras, cuando pienso
en lo que es la vida,
no puedo evitar de decírselo a Georgette,
a fin de comer algo agradable y salir,   25
por la tarde, comprar un buen periódico,
guardar un día para cuando no haya,
una noche también, para cuando haya
(así se dice en el Perú —me excuso);
del mismo modo, sufro con gran cuidado,   30
a fin de no gritar o de llorar, ya que los ojos
poseen, independientemente de uno, sus pobrezas,
quiero decir, su oficio, algo
que resbala del alma y cae al alma . . .

Habiendo atravesado   35

24.   *Georgette*: the poet's wife.

The fact of it is . . .

The fact of it is that the place where I put on
my trousers is a house where
I take off my shirt at the top of my voice
and where I have a floor, a soul, a map of my Spain.
Just now I was talking
about me to myself, and I placed
an enormous loaf of bread on top of a little book
and then I rang the changes, I shifted,
wanting to do a bit humming, the right
side of life over to the left;
later I washed myself, all of me, my belly,
vigorously, with dignity;
then I turned round to see what gets dirty,
I scraped what leads me on a tight leash
and I straightened the map which
was nodding or weeping, I don't know.

My house, unfortunately, is a house,
a floor, fortunately, where dwell
my beloved little spoon with its inscription,
my dear skeleton now unlettered,
my razor, a permanent cigarette.
Honestly, when I think
what life is,
I can't help mentioning it to Georgette,
so as to eat something nice and then go out,
in the evening, to buy a good newspaper,
to save a day for when there isn't one,
a night too for when there is
(sorry — it's what they say in Peru);
likewise, I suffer with great care,
so as not to scream or weep, for our eyes,
independently of one, have their weaknesses,
I mean their job, something
that slips from the soul and falls to the soul . . .

Having come through

quince años; después, quince, y, antes, quince,
uno se siente, en realidad, tontillo,
es natural, por lo demás ¡qué hacer!
¿Y qué dejar de hacer, que es lo peor?
Sino vivir, sino llegar   40
a ser lo que es uno entre millones
de panes, entre miles de vinos, entre cientos de bocas,
entre el sol y su rayo que es de luna
y entre la misa, el pan, el vino y mi alma.

Hoy es domingo, y por eso,   45
me viene a la cabeza la idea, al pecho el llanto
y a la garganta, así como un gran bulto.
Hoy es domingo, y esto
tiene muchos siglos; de otra manera,
sería, quizá, lunes, y vendríame al corazón la idea,   50
al seso, el llanto
y a la garganta, una gana espantosa de ahogar
lo que ahora siento,
como un hombre que soy y que he sufrido.

fifteen years, fifteen after that, and fifteen before,
one really feels foolish,
it's only natural; besides, what can one do?
Or stop doing, which is even worse?
Except to live, except to become
what one is among millions
of loaves of bread, among thousands of wines, among hundreds of mouths,
among the sun and its ray which is a moonbeam
and among the Mass, the bread, the wine and my soul.

Today is Sunday, and for that reason
the idea comes into my head, the sobbing into my breast
and into my throat a kind of great lump.
Today is Sunday, and this
is centuries old; otherwise,
it would maybe be Monday, and the idea would come into my heart,
the sobbing into my brain
and into my throat a frightful longing to stifle
what I feel now,
man that I am and having suffered as one.

ESPAÑA, APARTA DE MÍ ESTE CÁLIZ (1939)

Himno a los voluntarios de la República

Voluntario de España, miliciano
de huesos fidedignos, cuando marcha a morir tu corazón,
cuando marcha a matar con su agonía
mundial, no sé verdaderamente
qué hacer, dónde ponerme; corro, escribo, aplaudo,   5
lloro, atisbo, destrozo, apagan, digo
a mi pecho que acabe, al bien, que venga,
y quiero desgraciarme;
descúbrome la frente impersonal hasta tocar
el vaso de la sangre, me detengo,   10
detienen mi tamaño esas famosas caídas de arquitecto
con las que se honra el animal que me honra;
refluyen mis instintos a sus sogas,
humea ante mi tumba la alegría
y, otra vez, sin saber qué hacer, sin nada, déjame,   15
desde mi piedra en blanco, déjame,
solo,
cuadrumano, más acá, mucho más lejos,
al no caber entre mis manos tu largo rato extático,
quiebro contra tu rapidez de doble filo   20
mi pequeñez en traje de grandeza!

Un día diurno, claro, atento, fértil
¡oh bienio, el de los lóbregos semestres suplicantes,
por el que iba la pólvora mordiéndose los codos!
¡oh dura pena y más duros pedernales!   25
¡oh frenos los tascados por el pueblo!
Un día prendió el pueblo su fósforo cautivo, oró de cólera
y soberanamente pleno, circular,
cerró su natalicio con manos electivas;

---

23.   This is a reference to the years 1934-36, the so-called "Black Biennium" leading up to the Civil War.

24.   *morderse los codos* (Am.), to hold one's feelings in check.

SPAIN, TAKE THIS CUP FROM ME (1939)

Hymn to the Volunteers of the Republic

Volunteer of Spain, militiaman
of trustworthy bones, when your heart marches off to die,
when it marches off to kill with its world-wide
agony, I truly don't know
what to do, where to put myself; I run about, I write, I applaud,
I weep, I watch, I destroy, they extinguish, I tell
my breast to make an end to it, good, to come,
and I want to do myself injury;
I bare my impersonal forehead till I touch
the vessel of my blood, I restrain myself,
my stature is restrained by those famous architect's falls
which honour the animal which honours me;
my instincts ebb back to their halters,
joy smokes before my tomb
and, once again, not knowing what to do, with nothing, leave me
behind on my blank stone, leave me,
alone,
quadrumane, closer by, much more distant,
for my hands won't hold your long ecstatic moment
and I smash against your double-edged speed
my smallness dressed up in grandeur.

One diurnal day, clear, expectant, fertile
— oh biennium of gloomy, suppliant semesters
throughout which gunpowder kept biting its lip!
oh hard pain and harder flints!
oh bits champed by the people! —,
one day the people lit their captive match, prayed with rage
and sovereignly full, circular,
sealed their birthright with elective hands;

27-31. These lines refer to the victory of the Popular Front in the elections of February 1936.
29. *cerró su natalicio* is a somewhat ambiguous phrase which might alternatively be interpreted
as "brought to a close the condition into which they had been born".

107

arrastraban candado ya los déspotas 30
y en el candado, sus bacterias muertas ...

¿Batallas? ¡No! ¡Pasiones! Y pasiones precedidas
de dolores con rejas de esperanzas,
¡de dolores de pueblo con esperanzas de hombres!
¡Muerte y pasión de paz, las populares! 35
¡Muerte y pasión guerreras entre olivos, entendámonos!
Tal en tu aliento cambian de agujas atmosféricas los vientos
y de llave las tumbas en tu pecho,
tu frontal elevándose a primera potencia de martirio.

El mundo exclama: "¡Cosas de españoles!" Y es verdad. Consideremos, 40
durante una balanza, a quema ropa,
a Calderón, dormido sobre la cola de un anfibio muerto,
o a Cervantes, diciendo: "Mi reino es de este mundo, pero
también del otro": ¡punta y filo en dos papeles!
Contemplemos a Goya, de hinojos y rezando ante un espejo, 45
a Coll, el paladín en cuyo asalto cartesiano
tuvo un sudor de nube el paso llano,
o a Quevedo, ese abuelo instantáneo de los dinamiteros,
o a Cajal, devorado por su pequeño infinito, o todavía
a Teresa, mujer, que muere porque no muere, 50
o a Lina Odena, en pugna en más de un punto con Teresa ...
(Todo acto o voz genial viene del pueblo
y va hacia él, de frente o transmitido
por incesantes briznas, por el humo rosado
de amargas contraseñas sin fortuna.) 55
Así tu criatura, miliciano, así tu exangüe criatura,
agitada por una piedra inmóvil,
se sacrifica, apártase,
decae para arriba y por su llama incombustible sube,
sube hasta los débiles, 60
distribuyendo españas a los toros,
toros a las palomas ...

40-51. The writers Pedro Calderón de la Barca (1600-1681), Miguel de Cervantes Saavedra (1547-
1616) and Francisco de Quevedo y Villegas (1580-1645), the mystic Santa Teresa de Jesús
(1515-1582) and the painter Francisco de Goya (1746-1828) represent the Spanish cultural
tradition, as does Santiago Ramón y Cajal (1852-1943), a celebrated histologist who
specialised in the microscopic study of cells in the nervous system. Antonio Coll and Lina
Odena were Republican Civil War heroes: the former was renowned for his single-handed

the despots were now trailing padlocks
and in the padlocks their dead bacteria . . .

Battles? No! Passions! And passions preceded
by sorrows with bars of hope,
by sorrows of common people with hopes of men!
Death and passion for peace, the people's!
Martial death and passion among olive trees, let's be clear about it!
Thus in your breath the winds change atmospheric needle
and the tombs change key in your breast,
as your frontal raises itself to the first power of martyrdom.

The world exclaims: "One of those Spanish affairs!" And it's true. Let's consider,
in a balance, at point-blank range,
Calderón asleep on the tail of a dead amphibian,
or Cervantes saying, "My kingdom is of this world, but
also of the next": point and edge in two roles!
Let's observe Goya, on his knees and praying in front of a mirror,
Coll, the paladin in whose Cartesian assault
plain footsteps had a sweat of clouds,
or Quevedo, that instantaneous grandfather of the dynamiters,
or Cajal, devoured by his tiny infinite, or, again,
Teresa, a woman, dying because she doesn't die,
or Lina Odena, at odds with Teresa on more than one issue . . .
(Every act or voice of genius comes from the people
and goes towards them, directly or conveyed
by incessant blades of grass, by the rosy smoke
of bitter, unsuccessful passwords.)
Thus your creature, militiaman, your bloodless creature,
stirred by a motionless stone,
sacrifices itself, departs,
declines upwards and rises up its incombustible flame,
rises up to the weak,
distributing spains to the bulls,
bulls to the doves . . .

---

attack on Nationalist tanks, while the latter died on the southern front. Vallejo sees a
continuity linking these popular heroes with the great figures of Spanish culture in that both
embody the Spanish striving for the ideal, but at the same time these new heroes are viewed
as having superseded their predecessors by bringing the ideal down to earth and seeking it in
this world.

Proletario que mueres de universo, ¡en qué frenética armonía
acabará tu grandeza, tu miseria, tu vorágine impelente,
tu violencia metódica, tu caos teórico y práctico, tu gana   65
dantesca, españolísima, de amar, aunque sea a traición, a tu enemigo!
¡Liberador ceñido de grilletes,
sin cuyo esfuerzo hasta hoy continuaría sin asas la extensión,
vagarían acéfalos los clavos,
antiguo, lento, colorado, el día,   70
nuestros amados cascos, insepultos!
¡Campesino caído con tu verde follaje por el hombre,
con la inflexión social de tu meñique,
con tu buey que se queda, con tu física,
también con tu palabra atada a un palo   75
y tu cielo arrendado
y con la arcilla inserta en tu cansancio
y la que estaba en tu uña, caminando!
¡Constructores
agrícolas, civiles y guerreros,   80
de la activa, hormigueante eternidad: estaba escrito
que vosotros haríais la luz, entornando
con la muerte vuestros ojos;
que, a la caída cruel de vuestras bocas,
vendrá en siete bandejas la abundancia, todo   85
en el mundo será de oro súbito
y el oro,
fabulosos mendigos de vuestra propia secreción de sangre,
y el oro mismo será entonces de oro!

¡Se amarán todos los hombres   90
y comerán tomados de las puntas de vuestros pañuelos tristes
y beberán en nombre
de vuestras gargantas infaustas!
Descansarán andando al pie de esta carrera,
sollozarán pensando en vuestras órbitas, venturosos   95
serán y al son
de vuestro atroz retorno, florecido, innato,
ajustarán mañana sus quehaceres, sus figuras soñadas y cantadas!

¡Unos mismos zapatos irán bien al que asciende
sin vías a su cuerpo   100
y al que baja hasta la forma de su alma!

Proletarian dying of the universe, in what frantic harmony
will your greatness end, your misery, your driving maelstrom,
your methodical violence, your chaos theoretical and practical, your urge,
Dantesque and so very Spanish, to love your enemy, be it by treachery!
Liberator girded with fetters,
but for whose endeavour the expanse would still be handleless to this very day,
nails go about headless,
the day remain ancient, slow, red,
our beloved skulls, unburied!
Peasant fallen for man with your green foliage,
with the social inflection of your little finger,
with your ox that remains behind, with your physics,
also with your word tied to a stick
and your rented sky
and with the clay ingrained in your weariness
and that which was under your nails on the march!
Builders,
agricultural, civilian and military,
of bustling, teeming eternity: it was written
that you would create light, closing
your eyes with death;
that, with the cruel fall of your mouths,
abundance will come on seven salvers, everything
in the world will suddenly be of gold
and gold,
oh fabulous beggars of your own secretion of blood,
gold itself will then be of gold!

All men will love one another
and will eat holding the corners of your sad handkerchiefs
and will drink in the name
of your ill-fated throats!
They'll rest walking at the foot of this run
and they'll weep thinking of your orbits, happy
they'll be and to the sound
of your return, atrocious, flourishing, innate,
tomorrow they'll adjust their chores, the figures they've dreamt and sung!

The same shoes will fit him who ascends
without track to his body
and him who descends to the form of his soul!

¡Entrelazándose hablarán los mudos, los tullidos andarán!
¡Verán, ya de regreso, los ciegos
y palpitando escucharán los sordos!
¡Sabrán los ignorantes, ignorarán los sabios!   105
¡Serán dados los besos que no pudisteis dar!
¡Sólo la muerte morirá! ¡La hormiga
traerá pedacitos de pan al elefante encadenado
a su brutal delicadeza; volverán
los niños abortados a nacer perfectos, espaciales   110
y trabajarán todos los hombres,
engendrarán todos los hombres,
comprenderán todos los hombres!

¡Obrero, salvador, redentor nuestro,
perdónanos, hermano, nuestras deudas!   115
Como dice un tambor al redoblar, en sus adagios:
¡qué jamás tan efímero, tu espalda!
¡qué siempre tan cambiante, tu perfil!

¡Voluntario italiano, entre cuyos animales de batalla
un león abisinio va cojeando!   120
¡Voluntario soviético, marchando a la cabeza de tu pecho universal!
¡Voluntarios del sur, del norte, del oriente
y tú, el occidental, cerrando el canto fúnebre del alba!
¡Soldado conocido, cuyo nombre
desfila en el sonido de un abrazo!   125
¡Combatiente que la tierra criara, armándote
de polvo,
calzándote de imanes positivos,
vigentes tus creencias personales,
distinto de carácter, íntima tu férula,   130
el cutis inmediato,
andándote tu idioma por los hombros
y el alma coronada de guijarros!
¡Voluntario fajado de tu zona fría,
templada o tórrida,   135
héroes a la redonda,
víctima en columna de vencedores:
en España, en Madrid, están llamando

120.   This is an allusion to Mussolini's invasion of Abyssinia which preceded the Spanish Civil
       War and which drove the Emperor, the so-called "Lion of Judea", into exile. It is implied that

112

Embracing, the dumb will speak, the lame will walk!
The returning blind will see
and, quivering, the deaf will hear!
The ignorant will be wise, the wise ignorant!
Given will be the kisses you couldn't give!
Only death will die! The ant
will bring scraps of bread to the elephant fettered
to its brutal delicacy; aborted children
will be born again, perfect, spatial,
and all men will work,
all men will procreate,
all men will understand!

Worker, saviour, our redeemer,
forgive us, brother, our trespasses!
As a rolling drum says in its adagios:
what an ephemeral never, your back!
what a changing always, your profile!

Italian volunteer, among whose campaign animals
limps an Abyssinian lion!
Soviet volunteer, marching at the head of your universal breast!
Volunteers from the south, from the north, from the east
and you, the westerner, bringing up the rear of the dawn's funeral chant!
Known soldier, whose name
parades in the sound of an embrace!
Combatant whom the earth raised, arming you
with dust,
shoeing you with positive magnets,
you, with your personal beliefs in full force,
your distinct character, your intimate rod,
your immediate complexion,
your language walking about on your shoulders
and your soul crowned with pebbles!
Volunteer swathed in your cold,
temperate or torrid zone,
heroes all round,
victim in a column of victors:
in Spain, in Madrid, they're calling you

in struggling against Fascism in Spain the Italian volunteers are also fighting the cause of
wounded Abyssinia, the victim of their own country's Fascist dictatorship.

a matar, voluntarios de la vida!

Porque en España matan, otros matan   140
al niño, a su juguete que se para,
a la madre Rosenda esplendorosa,
al viejo Adán que hablaba en alta voz con su caballo
y al perro que dormía en la escalera.
¡Matan al libro, tiran a sus verbos auxiliares,   145
a su indefensa página primera!
Matan el caso exacto de la estatua,
al sabio, a su bastón, a su colega,
al barbero de al lado —me cortó posiblemente,
pero buen hombre y, luego, infortunado;   150
al mendigo que ayer cantaba enfrente,
a la enfermera que hoy pasó llorando,
al sacerdote a cuestas con la altura tenaz de sus rodillas . . .

¡Voluntarios,
por la vida, por los buenos, matad   155
a la muerte, matad a los malos!
¡Hacedlo por la libertad de todos,
del explotado y del explotador,
por la paz indolora —la sospecho
cuando duermo al pie de mi frente   160
y más cuando circulo dando voces—
y hacedlo, voy diciendo,
por el analfabeto a quien escribo,
por el genio descalzo y su cordero,
por los camaradas caídos,   165
sus cenizas abrazadas al cadáver de un camino!

Para que vosotros,
voluntarios de España y del mundo, vinierais,
soñé que era yo bueno, y era para ver
vuestra sangre, voluntarios . . .   170
De esto hace mucho pecho, muchas ansias,
muchos camellos en edad de orar.
Marcha hoy de vuestra parte el bien ardiendo,
os siguen con cariño los reptiles de pestaña inmanente
y, a dos pasos, a uno,   175
la dirección del agua que corre a ver su límite antes que arda.

to kill, volunteers of life!

Because they're killing in Spain, others kill
the child, his toy which comes to a stop,
radiant mother Rosenda,
old Adam who talked aloud with his horse,
and the dog which slept on the stairs.
They kill the book, they fire on its auxiliary verbs,
on its defenceless first page!
They kill the statue's exact case,
the scholar, his stick, his colleague,
the barber next door — possibly he cut me,
but a good man and, besides, unfortunate;
the beggar who yesterday was singing opposite,
the nurse who today went by weeping,
the priest burdened with the persistent height of his knees . . .

Volunteers,
for life, for good men, kill
death, kill the wicked!
Do it for the freedom of everyone,
of the exploited and of the exploiter,
for peace without pain — I intuit it
when I'm asleep at the foot of my forehead
and even more when I go around shouting —,
and do it, I say,
for the illiterate to whom I write,
for the barefoot genius and his lamb,
for the comrades who have fallen,
their ashes embracing the corpse of a road!

So that you
would come, volunteers of Spain and the world,
I dreamt that I was good, and it was to see
your blood, volunteers . . .
That was much breast ago, many yearnings,
many camels at the age of prayer.
Today good marches blazing on your side,
there follow you lovingly reptiles with immanent eyelashes
and, two steps, one step behind,
the course of water rushing to see its limit before it burns.

Los mendigos ...

Los mendigos pelean por España,
mendigando en París, en Roma, en Praga
y refrendando así, con mano gótica, rogante,
los pies de los Apóstoles, en Londres, en New York, en Méjico.
Los pordioseros luchan suplicando infernalmente   5
a Dios por Santander,
la lid en que ya nadie es derrotado.
Al sufrimiento antiguo
danse, encarnízanse en llorar plomo social
al pie del individuo,   10
y atacan a gemidos, los mendigos,
matando con tan sólo ser mendigos.

Ruegos de infantería,
en que el arma ruega del metal para arriba,
y ruega la ira, más acá de la pólvora iracunda.   15
Tácitos escuadrones que disparan,
con cadencia mortal, su mansedumbre,
desde un umbral, desde sí mismos, ¡ay! desde sí mismos.
Potenciales guerreros
sin calcetines al calzar el trueno,   20
satánicos, numéricos,
arrastrando sus títulos de fuerza,
migaja al cinto,
fusil doble calibre: sangre y sangre.
¡El poeta saluda al sufrimiento armado!   25

116

beggar can cause a change in your perception of world + hence behaviour.

The beggars ...

marxism:
Beggar is a living illustration of defect in capitalism

But more a Xian image:

The beggars are fighting for Spain,
begging in Paris, in Rome, in Prague
and thus seconding, with an imploring Gothic hand,
the feet of the Apostles, in London, in New York, in Mexico City.
The beggars fight with their infernal supplications
to God on behalf of Santander,
the conflict in which no longer is anyone defeated.
They abandon themselves
to their ancient suffering, they remorselessly weep social lead
at the foot of the individual,
and they attack with moans, do the beggars,
killing by merely being beggars.

Pleas of infantry
in which the weapon pleads from the metal upwards
and anger pleads this side of the irate gunpowder.
Tacit squadrons firing
their meekness, with mortal cadence,
from a threshold, from themselves, oh, from their very selves.
Potential warriors
with sockless feet shod in thunder,
satanical, numerical,
dragging the titles of their strength,
a crumb at the belt, — *breaks rythm*
a double-calibre rifle: blood and blood.
The poet salutes armed suffering!

awkward alliteration + rythm   3 pies ...
20 — calcetines

Suffering is sacrifice, will bring salvation ie justice
secular use of X images/ideas — deconstructs the
language — reader has to view it in new light.

Free verse — no mechanical regularity. —
author doesn't want it to be aesthetically pleasing 117
wants us to think.

Masa

Al fin de la batalla,
y muerto el combatiente, vino hacia él un hombre
y le dijo: "¡No mueras; te amo tanto!"
Pero el cadáver ¡ay! siguió muriendo.

Se le acercaron dos y repitiéronle: 5
"¡No nos dejes! ¡Valor! ¡Vuelve a la vida!"
Pero el cadáver ¡ay! siguió muriendo.

Acudieron a él veinte, cien, mil, quinientos mil,
clamando: "¡Tanto amor, y no poder nada contra la muerte!"
Pero el cadáver ¡ay! siguió muriendo.   10

Le rodearon millones de individuos,
con un ruego común: "¡Quédate, hermano!"
Pero el cadáver ¡ay! siguió muriendo.

Entonces, todos los hombres de la tierra
le rodearon; les vio el cadáver triste, emocionado;   15
incorporóse lentamente,
abrazó al primer hombre; echóse a andar . . .

Mass

At the end of the battle,
as the combatant lay dead, a man came up to him
and said: "Don't die, I love you so much!"
But the corpse, alas!, kept on dying.

Two men approached him and said the same thing:
"Don't leave us! Courage! Come back to life!"
But the corpse, alas!, kept on dying.

Twenty came to him, a hundred, a thousand, five hundred thousand,
all crying out: "So much love and to be powerless against death!"
But the corpse, alas!, kept on dying.

Millions of individuals surrounded him,
with a common plea: "Stay with us, brother!"
But the corpse, alas!, kept on dying.

Then all the men on earth surrounded him;
the corpse looked at them sadly, deeply moved;
he got up slowly,
embraced the first man; began to walk . . .

ESPAÑA, APARTA DE MÍ ESTE CÁLIZ

España, aparta de mí este cáliz

Niños del mundo,
si cae España —digo, es un decir—
si cae
del cielo abajo su antebrazo que asen,
en cabestro, dos láminas terrestres;   5
niños, ¡qué edad la de las sienes cóncavas!
¡qué temprano en el sol lo que os decía!
¡qué pronto en vuestro pecho el ruido anciano!
¡qué viejo vuestro 2 en el cuaderno!

¡Niños del mundo, está   10
la madre España con su vientre a cuestas;
está nuestra maestra con sus férulas,
está madre y maestra,
cruz y madera, porque os dio la altura,
vértigo y división y suma, niños;   15
está con ella, padres procesales!

Si cae —digo, es un decir— si cae
España, de la tierra para abajo,
niños, ¡cómo vais a cesar de crecer!
¡cómo va a castigar el año al mes!   20
¡cómo van a quedarse en diez los dientes,
en palote el diptongo, la medalla en llanto!
¡Cómo va el corderillo a continuar
atado por la pata al gran tintero!
¡Cómo vais a bajar las gradas del alfabeto   25
hasta la letra en que nació la pena!

Niños,
hijos de los guerreros, entretanto,
bajad la voz, que España está ahora mismo repartiendo
la energía entre el reino animal,   30
las florecillas, los cometas y los hombres.
¡Bajad la voz, que está
con su rigor, que es grande, sin saber
qué hacer, y está en su mano

120

Spain, Take This Cup From Me

Children of the world,
if Spain should fall — I'm just supposing —,
if her forearm
should fall from the sky gripped
in the halter of two terrestrial sheets;
children, what an age, that of the concave temples!
how early in the sun what I was telling you!
how soon the old noise in your chest!
how old your 2 in your notebook!

Children of the world,
mother Spain is shouldering the burden of her womb;
she's our teacher with her birches,
she's mother and teacher,
cross and wood, for she gave you height,
vertigo and division and addition, children;
it rests with her, judicial parents!

If Spain should fall — I'm just supposing —,
if she should fall from the earth downwards,
children, how you are going to stop growing!
how the year is going to punish the month!
how your teeth will remain at ten,
the dipthong in downstroke, the medal in tears!
How the little lamb will remain
tethered by the leg to the great inkwell!
How you are going to descend the steps of the alphabet
to the letter where grief was born!

Children,
children of the warriors, in the meantime
lower your voices, for at this moment Spain is distributing
her energy among the animal kingdom,
the small flowers, the comets and men.
Lower your voices, for she's
in her hardship, which is great, not knowing
what to do, and in her hand is

+ Rep. falls — ed will be affected — an unusual take on issue?

121

la calavera hablando y habla y habla,   35
la calavera, aquélla de la trenza,
la calavera, aquélla de la vida! *paradox*

¡Bajad la voz, os digo;
bajad la voz, el canto de las sílabas, el llanto
de la materia y el rumor menor de las pirámides, y aún   40
el de las sienes que andan con dos piedras!
¡Bajad el aliento, y si
el antebrazo baja,
si las férulas suenan, si es la noche,
si el cielo cabe en dos limbos terrestres,   45
si hay ruido en el sonido de las puertas,
si tardo,
si no veis a nadie, si os asustan
los lápices sin punta, si la madre
España cae —digo, es un decir—   50
salid, niños del mundo; id a buscarla! ...

universal mother — socialist society.

themes:
religion, orphanhood, madre E, V's hopes for future

Religion — Father, take this cup from me (in Gethsemane)
in a moment of weakness — V is despairing fearing defeat.
V as a prophet — but man is the saviour (Com. background)
Orphanhood (3 + 23 of Trilce) — 'La madre E': V is Peruvian.
V sees itas a worldwide confrontation of fascism + communism.

Hopes — hopeful feeling at end even if Spain falls/rev fails

Devices — a hymn, in structure — voice raised in exaltation.
school refs (he was a teacher).
Style + lang. quite accessible (addressing people)
repeti. reiterative ennumeration line 3 → line 44 →

Metrics — Free verse (no regularity, no rhyme)
— a political speech? a sermon?

Historical events → humanities struggle to build a
better world
(is transformed into)

the skull, talking and talking and talking,
that skull with the tress,
that skull of life!

Lower your voices, I tell you;
lower your voices, the chant of the syllables, the weeping
of matter and the lesser murmur of the pyramids, and even
that of the temples which function with two stones!
Lower your breath, and if
the forearm descends,
if the birches sound, if it is night,
if the sky fits into two terrestrial limbos,
if there's noise in the sound of the doors,
if I'm late,
if you don't see anyone, if blunt pencils
frighten you, if mother
Spain should fall — I'm just supposing — ,
go out, children of the world; go out and look for her! ...

Communist writes obligation (they might feel)
to end positively — other warriors take up guns
is a common idea but historically it did happen —
Alliance was WWII even though Spanish
didn't)

not purely Sp. conflict
— 'universal fight' — a reasonable way of seeing
conflict (2nd WW followed it)

123

INDEX OF FIRST LINES

INDEX OF FIRST LINES